WEALTH WITHOUT CASH

WEALTH WITHOUT CASH

Supercharge Your Real
Estate Investing with
Subject-To, Seller Financing,
and Other Creative Deals

PACE MORBY

BiggerPockets®
PUBLISHING
Denver, Colorado

Praise for
WEALTH WITHOUT CASH

"There's a reason that Pace Morby is considered the 'GOAT' (greatest of all time). His knowledge is second to none, but even more importantly, his transparency and willingness to share and teach others is something that is one of a kind… His strategy not only works but is also replicable by new and seasoned investors alike."

—VEENA JETTI, Founding partner of Vive Funds,
***Forbes* councilmember, and multifamily investor**

"You should read this book… not because Pace Morby is one of the smartest creative finance experts on the planet. Not because Pace Morby has created a legacy of generational wealth for his family. You should read this book because Pace didn't write it for himself. He wrote it for *you*."

—HENRY WASHINGTON, Author, real estate investor,
and co-host of BiggerPockets *On the Market* podcast

Wealth without Cash: Supercharge Your Real Estate Investing with Subject-To, Seller Financing, and Other Creative Deals
Pace Morby

Published by BiggerPockets Publishing LLC, Denver, CO
Copyright © 2023 by Pace Morby
All rights reserved.

Publisher's Cataloging-in-Publication Data
Names: Morby, Pace, author.
Title: Wealth without cash : supercharge your real estate investing with subject-to , seller financing , and other creative deals / by Pace Morby.
Description: Denver, CO: BiggerPockets Publishing, 2023.
Identifiers: LCCN: 2022947410 | ISBN: 9781947200883 (hardcover) | 9781947200890 (ebook)
Subjects: LCSH Real estate investment--Finance. | Real estate business--United States--Finance. | Mortgage loans--United States. | Housing--Finance. | Small business--Finance. | BISAC BUSINESS & ECONOMICS / Real Estate / General | BUSINESS & ECONOMICS / Real Estate / Mortgages | BUSINESS & ECONOMICS / Investments & Securities / Real Estate
Classification: LCC HD1375.B68.M67 2023 | DDC 658.1/5--dc23

Printed on recycled paper in the United States of America
VP 10 9 8 7 6 5 4 3 2 1

Dedication

To my wife, Laura, and our children,
Asher, Corbin, and Monday.

Table of Contents

Introduction

When I was a kid, wealth didn't seem attainable. As the third of twelve children, many of my weeks were just about survival. If you were a few minutes late for breakfast, you didn't eat. If you needed something other than your next meal, you had to figure out how to make your own money to buy it. We were loved, don't get me wrong, but my parents were so busy making ends meet, they didn't have time to think about any other way to get by. My mom brought in money selling handmade items and Dad was always self-employed. He worked two jobs. One job was always on the side. This is how he made enough to support all of us. He couldn't buy a house in a traditional manner, so he had to get creative to keep a roof over his family's head. In some ways, that explains why we moved twenty-six times before I turned 19 years old. Dad was using methods I now use today for investment properties, as creative finance is everywhere, but he was too busy working to realize he could make real money based on the knowledge he already had.

Dad never really found a way to build a profitable system. He knew how to start—and start over—but not how to scale. Whenever he built a new business, he would grow to a point beyond a single person's capabilities and then it would come tumbling down like a house of cards. He'd move to a new state and find a new opportunity, hauling with him thirteen mouths that needed to be fed. When he did reach out for help, he would find a partner who thought exactly like him rather than someone who could multiply his strengths and minimize his weaknesses. It was never a work ethic problem—my dad simply lacked the correct information.

My parents taught me how to work hard but not how to work smart. I give them all the credit for my work ethic; I challenge anyone to put in more hours than my family or serve more people than we did growing up. But that doesn't mean we weren't often on a hamster wheel.

The problem with learning to work hard is that everyone learns to work hard. It's how you survive. But survival isn't enough. For starters, you never get a break. When you live paycheck to paycheck or month to month, it's a relentless grind—and in the end, the grind will win. Ironically, it's more difficult to work hard than pursue wealth. The problem is that parents who aren't wealthy teach their children to work hard, because that's all they know how to teach them. "Work harder and it will pay off." Sure, working hard is important, but in the right areas.

Every time I asked my dad for advice, he told me to work harder. That's all he knew, and that's all he still knows today. He works fifty to eighty hours every week, even though he's well into retirement age. "Take on more clients. Work Saturdays and Sundays. Do whatever you have to do," he would tell me. He prides himself in his work. I'm the same way, but my focus is different.

I bet a lot of you are in the same place; maybe you feel like you're in survival mode right now. It's a path I followed. We react to small fires every day, rather than taking a moment to pursue another path, one that can lead us to either some extra money each month or true generational wealth. Whichever road you want to follow, it all starts by looking for the bunnies.

Looking for the Bunnies

I was following in Dad's footsteps, running a construction business. My team had finished about 7,000 jobs, flipping houses for early giants like Opendoor, Offerpad, and Zillow. That's when I met Bethany Willis. It was our third job together and I had showed up about thirty minutes early to make sure everything was set up for the day and the team was on time. Bethany arrived a few minutes later. We had a good rapport. Over the steam of morning coffee and an array of tools, she changed my life.

"You're always thirty minutes early," she said. "You're articulate. You're unlike many of the other contractors I've worked with. Why are you working for me?" I was as puzzled as I was flattered by the statement. I told her the usual: how much I enjoyed the work and how I was glad to be in the real estate business. But here's where she stopped me. Here's where she opened up my mind in a new way. "Pace, you're not in the real estate business. You work for me. I'm in the real estate business. You're in the service business. That's what I'm saying. You're on-site, sure, but you're a service provider to the business, like a mobile notary, a lender, a title company, or even a Realtor. The only people actually in the real estate business are investors. Where you're at now, you're a Google search away from being replaced."

I wasn't blind. I knew real estate investors were generally in a position to make the most money, but I had never thought about my work as merely a service to someone else. It hit me like a ton of bricks. I think I politely defended my position as we finished our coffee, but I knew she was right. That day was a bit of a whirlwind. I continued all of my daily work, but that night when I got home, everything was suddenly different. I talked to my wife, Laura, over dinner in our rented home. My mind was racing. I was circling around an inevitable conclusion that Laura confirmed for me. I was in the wrong business.

The next time Bethany stopped by the job site, we shared some small talk, but I soon interrupted with some questions she had been waiting for: How do I get started? How do I do it myself? She somewhat smiled as I fired off a series of questions, ones that had been holding me back. I felt like I didn't know where the money came from. "Private lenders. Hard money," she casually responded. "How do I know if it's a deal? How do I evaluate and compare properties and make an offer?" Again, she quickly filled in the blanks, but I could tell she wasn't interested in just teaching me lessons. She wanted to fill in enough just so I would start. "Pace, I'm happy to give you all of the advice you need, but not like this. I can't just teach you a history lesson. It's not school. You have to take a little bit, use it, then come back for more. You don't need to know every single step. You just need to know the next step." That was the best advice I had heard in my life. It's the goal of this book. It's also what led me to the bunnies.

I took Bethany's advice. She told me there were countless ways to generate leads, but we'd start with a simple one I could do in my spare time. She taught me how to send postcards. Personally, this isn't something I teach because it can get expensive and I like for people to start with little to no money, but it's what worked at the time. I got online and found people in the areas I liked who had a lot of equity in their homes, and I paid a company to send out postcards for me expressing my interest in buying their homes. After a few days, I started getting some phone calls from the postcards. I was so busy working that I missed the first two phone calls—carrying toilets when I should have been answering calls to true wealth. After missing the first two calls, I committed to never missing another. The third call was a woman named Janney. She was a retired teacher who wanted to move back to Oregon. I didn't know it at the time, but this phone call would change the trajectory of my life.

I had a good conversation with Janney, but I quickly realized I was out of steps and needed to consult with Bethany. I told Janney I wanted to talk with a partner and that I would get back to her as soon as possible. I explained Janney's situation to Bethany and she told me to set up a face-to-face meeting with the seller so I could make a cash offer, which I now know is a form of wholesaling. I hesitated once again, not knowing what kind of offer I should make, but Bethany promised to help me out with that as well. While I was driving to meet the seller, Bethany looked at comparable properties (comps) on her end and told me I should offer $150,000 for the house. I asked a few more questions, which she happily answered, and then I made my way to meet the seller at the house. I still didn't know exactly where she got this number from, but I didn't let lack of knowledge stop me. I trusted her and continued to the next step.

Janney, the seller, told me a little more about her situation. After some small talk and a quick walk around the property, I told her the sentence I had been practicing in my head. "I'm sure you're talking to other investors, but what has kept you from selling so far?" She said that as a retired teacher, every penny mattered, but she also wanted to move quickly rather than put any more money into the home for repairs. That's when she said something that made my heart drop. "I've actually already got an offer for $165,000 but I'm meeting with a few more people to see if I can get a better offer."

I felt a little defeated. Bethany told me my cap was $150,000, but I knew Janney wouldn't take the offer if it meant losing $15,000 on the deal. I knew investing wasn't going to be easy, but I felt like I had gone down the right path and taken all the right turns. I told Janney the number I felt comfortable with was a little lower. "I'm afraid I'm not your buyer," I said. We started to walk back toward my car when she revealed a few more things about herself. It was hard to believe she was navigating all of this alone. She was selling her home without any help and talking to all of these potential buyers alone. "Even though I'm probably not your buyer, is there anything I can do to help?" I asked her.

She politely waved me off, but I pushed a little harder. "Look, teachers were always some of my favorite people growing up. I know there's probably not a deal here for me, but seriously, you've got a lot going on, is there any little thing I can do to help? Do you need help moving any of these boxes or anything like that?" There was a pause so I continued. "I'm from a family of twelve kids and I was an Eagle Scout growing up," I said with a smile. "Stuff like this was always a team effort, so yes, seriously, if there's anything I can do to help, I'm here." She was so surprised by the offer, but after I pushed a little more, she finally relented.

"Eagle Scout? You really just want to help? If you're serious, there is one thing I could use some help with. It's in the backyard. It's a bit unusual . . . ."

We walked around to the back of the house and that's when I saw her problem. There were three massive Flemish bunnies, like you would see in those Cadbury commercials. "I don't know what to do about these bunnies," she told me. "My granddaughter bought them for me, and I can't take them with me, and I can't just give them away without knowing they're going to a good home." It was unusual but I knew just who to call. I pulled out my phone and called up my mom. I told her about the situation on speakerphone, let her ask any questions to Janney, and, that day, Mom drove up there. She must have called a friend from church, because she showed up in a red truck I'd never seen before or since. But that was Mom—resourceful as ever. She picked up the bunnies and took them back to her small farm. Janney gave me a hug and I went back to my car. I didn't get the deal, but I did help her with her problem. It felt great.

I called Bethany on my way home and explained everything. Bethany told me, "That's amazing. You'll learn this whole business is helping people and solving problems. It's never about the house. If you can understand that, that's all you need to know." I loved that advice. I wrote it down and used it as wallpaper on my phone for years.

But here's the amazing part. About two weeks later, Janney calls and tells me she wants to sell me the house. "Janney, I appreciate that, but I can't do $165,000," I told her. Then she really shocked me.

She said, "I've decided to sell the house to you. I did get other offers around $165,000 but no one else took the time to care about me. No one else listened to me. No one else wanted to hear what was going on in my life. You did that for me and I haven't been able to stop thinking about your generosity. You selflessly helped me when there was nothing to gain and you're the type of person I want to do business with. I don't care what your number is, come up to my house and let's do the paperwork."

I was astounded. We talked a little more at her house and I then told her the price Bethany said I should offer. We agreed on $150,000 for the house. In fact, she told me she thought my number was going to be lower since I didn't say a number before. I called Bethany to share the good news and she walked me through the purchase agreement. As Bethany continued to talk, I asked her what I should do next. I was shocked once again that day. Bethany offered to buy the $150,000 house for $175,000, which would give me a $25,000 profit just for closing the deal. She could buy the deal from me, fix-and-flip it, then make additional money on the house. "Ask another question, take another step," she said when I picked my jaw up off the floor. I couldn't believe it. I just made $25,000 in about seven hours of work on my first wholesale deal and everyone was happy. It's all about the bunnies.

The Next Step, Not Every Step

I was hooked. I had learned a few things and I was eager to get leads and hopefully make some more deals. But when you do wholesale deals, a lot of people will want more money than you can give them, especially if they don't have equity in their homes. At the time, I just figured anything that didn't fit my wholesale criteria was a bad lead. I was spending a few hundred dollars per incoming phone call to acquire all of those "bad leads." About one third of the people didn't have equity, but they were in foreclosure and needed help. Someone had died, they had lost a job, or some other unfortunate situation had befallen them. I saw the same story time and time again. They needed to sell the house, but no Realtor could help them because there wasn't enough money for the Realtor or the bank to take their cut. In many cases, the seller would have to cut a check just to get out of a bad investment and avoid foreclosure. I wanted to help, so I sat down with an escrow officer and, honestly, she also changed my life.

I was using Facebook ads, sending postcards, and cold-calling foreclosures when I met Eileen Brown. I had made a little money wholesaling, but I still didn't know anything about creative finance. One day, I went to Eileen to open escrow on a deal I was working on and discuss some options. I had no idea how valuable she was going to be to my entire operation and overall mindset. I happened to explain a situation where I would normally just disqualify a lead. She told me, "Pace, you've been coming in here and working hard and you seem excited, but how's it going?" I told her I should have started this about 7,000 renovations earlier, but this was the position I was in. I told her I wanted to help out some of these people in foreclosure, but the numbers just didn't make sense.

"Why don't you just buy the house subject-to?" she asked me. I had never heard of this before. Neither she nor I had any idea the effect that her one little question would have on my life and the lives of so many others. She continued, "They don't need equity if you buy the house subject-to. You can give them what they want for the house." I had no idea what she was talking about, but I knew she had been doing creative finance deals for over forty years, so I kept asking questions, trying to wrap my head around what she was saying.

"What's that?" I asked.

"I've seen these scenarios for years," she said. "But look, here's what we can do. You keep taking action. You keep doing deals. There's no point in me telling you a bunch of stuff and then you trying to navigate it all. Instead, just keep making deals, bring me the deals, and I'll tell you how to structure them with creative finance."

Eileen's vow of support was all I needed to hear. She pushed me in the same way Bethany had pushed me. Take action. Figure it out along the way. You don't need every step, just the next step. I followed her instructions. I got out in my market and started creating problems, just like she told me to. But Eileen wasn't going to baby me too much. She told me not to call unless I had a deal. She didn't want hypotheticals. She wanted to solve real problems. "I only want to give you important information," she said. "I don't want to give you interesting information to ponder and think about. Go create scenarios. Next time you meet a seller with no equity or who wants too much money, tell them you have a solution." She was a real mentor for me. She gave me the most guidance and did so in the quickest fashion. She said, "Pace, go create as many problems as you can and come to me. I'll solve your problems."

That's exactly what I did. All of a sudden, I saw solvable problems everywhere. It's like when you buy a new car and suddenly you see the same car everywhere you go. I think this is how manifestation works. It's not so much magic as it is clarity. Eileen taught me that to be active in real estate was the quickest way to learn. You can't just spend time on YouTube and figure it out. You have to put yourself in real-world situations with real problems and then figure out how to solve those problems. I was so excited that I started to share some of these ideas on social media. I talked about what I had discovered and what Eileen had taught me and what I learned. Then, out of nowhere, people started sending me their so-called "dead leads" because they didn't know what to do with them (today about 60 percent of my deals come from dead leads).

Investors with my old mindset were disqualifying leads that didn't work for wholesale or their buy box (aka the type of deal they prefer to purchase) and marking them as dead ends. They didn't know what to do with them. Thanks to Eileen, I acquired about one hundred rentals over the span of just a few years from other investors' dead leads. And now, after fifteen years in the business, I have transacted on $250 million in real estate and acquired over 1,000 doors nationwide. I own over twenty active businesses as a majority stakeholder with nearly 700 employees. It's safe to say I know what I'm talking about when it comes to creative finance. Despite what Dave Ramsey might recommend, I never used my own money again. I never even had to use my own credit. It's been eighteen years since anyone pulled my credit for anything.

Whenever I talk to sellers, I always look for their version of Janney's bunnies. Over thousands of transactions, I've learned that every seller has a reason why they'll sell to you instead of someone else. There's a reason they'll sell at a discount or work with your terms or some other unique scenario. Your goal is to find the bunnies and solve their unsolvable problems. When you shift your mindset, you'll start to see problems and solutions in nearly every scenario. You might still not think this is possible. I didn't either until I started to close deals. But it's only impossible if you view it as a multistep process that you've never done before. You just need to solve the next step. Then the next one. As for the rest of it, all of the information you need is here. You just need to change the way you look at the problem. You need to start thinking creatively. Then the opportunities will come to you.

Speaking of a mindset shift, here's the craziest thing that happened during all of this: I called my dad and told him what I was doing. He knew I was in real estate because Mom had picked up those bunnies, and he knew I'd made $25,000 on my first deal. As I told him about sub-to and creative finance, I asked him, "Did you know this stuff existed?"

He replied, "How do you think I could afford every house you ever lived in?" This shocked me. Dad had been buying creatively but never shared that knowledge, because he thought it was more important that his kids work harder than everyone else to get ahead. Like I said, he had the knowledge but not the mindset to put that knowledge to work beyond survival. Today, at age 65, my dad is still living in a seller-financed home and prides himself on working hard every day. To this day, as a kitchen remodeler, he pours his energy, gifts, charisma, and work into other people's houses rather than into building his own wealth.

Don't read this book and continue the journey you're on. Don't spend years or decades climbing a ladder that's leaning on the wrong wall. Change your path and adjust your mindset. All the information you need to take your first step is here in the pages of this book, waiting for you to begin your journey to wealth.

And if, at the end of all this, you find yourself craving more creative finance content, go to www.biggerpockets.com/creativewealth for free videos, podcast episodes, blogs, downloadables, and more. Ready to begin?

CHAPTER 1

What Is *CREATIVE FINANCE* and Why Should You Care About It?

"Got nothin' but love for you / And all I wanted was for you to have a better life than I had."

—TUPAC, "LETTER 2 MY UNBORN"

There are only three ways to make money in real estate.

1. You can do wholesale.
2. You can do fix-and-flips or development.
3. You can buy and hold to build a long-term portfolio.

That's it. Everything else is a service or some form of these three options. But most people only see themselves as working within one of these three categories. With creative finance, you have the ability to master all three. Creative finance amplifies your opportunities because you can solve more problems than a competitor who only uses cash deals or other one-trick ponies who tread water in this business. And here's the other good news: You don't have to be an expert to get started.

With creative finance, you can get started faster but you can also improve over time. This is because every time you do a deal or learn a new skill, you can add another tool to your tool kit. Can you find another way to locate a seller's bunnies and solve their unsolvable problems, like how I solved Janney's bunny problem in the introduction? Honestly, for me, it's an addiction. I can't help but see distressed properties when I ride around or see problems that can be solved with creative finance when I pick up the phone.

I became an expert after I started to generate leads. Like baseball, it's all about how many times you get up to the plate. The more opportunities that come across the plate, the better you get. We'll go over the five ways to find deals a little later, in Chapter 7, but for now, just know that if you don't have leads you don't have a business. As you start to develop leads, you can start to dominate your local market.

When Eileen first started helping me close creative finance deals, I started to share these secrets on social media. I was amazed that I had never heard of these methods, and many of my early followers had never heard of them either. It got to the point where I could pull up in front of a house, share on social media that I was about to go in and talk to a potential buyer, and the competition would message me and say, "Ahh, I was there three days ago, I wish you weren't going in behind me." They knew I had more tools in my tool kit and had a better chance of solving the seller's problem to close the deal.

Every potential deal is a job site. If you show up with a hammer, you're just looking for nails. The hammer is the wholesale buyer. They've got cash and a lowball offer, but that's it. Some buyers take the offer because they really need the money. But others might be open to terms, especially if you explain how it works to them. Like you and me and many of my early followers, they've never heard of any of this before. You need to explain it simply so they know it's a win-win for both parties.

If you just show up with a hammer, all you can do is pound nails. But if you have a hammer and a screw gun and an air compressor, you can handle multiple types of jobs. I can do X, Y, and Z because I'm here to solve all sorts of problems. I'm not trying to adapt a seller to the one thing I do. No one needs a hammer when the job requires concrete.

Hopefully this is all making sense and it's clearer that creative finance isn't just some fly-by-night get-rich-quick scheme. Even if you get your first deal closed today, it could take ninety days to get paid for it. With creative finance, it's a short-term strategy and a long-term strategy built into one. Yes, you can buy a vacation home or a family home with the tools in this book. But you can also build an empire of 1,000 doors. Ironically, you need the same information to do either because the path to 1,000 doors starts with your first deal.

These are strategies that anyone can do. I've seen people in foreclosure figure out ways to get themselves out of foreclosure with creative finance. I've seen retired people quit their jobs and make more money as an investor after retirement than they made in forty years of work. I've seen 18-year-old kids buy rental properties while attending college. I've seen single moms build creative finance empires while working from home. It's all possible with creative finance.

Hopefully, this isn't coming off too cheesy. I used to see those late-night infomercial guys talking about low-money-down or no-money-down deals and I thought it was nonsense. I mean, Dave Ramsey says I need to save up all the money to pay cash, right? Everyone thinks it's too good to be true in the beginning, but there's a reason why it's sold this way. Creative finance goes against the grain. The majority of the market is built on banks and Realtors, two groups that can be cut out of many of these deals entirely. I do work with some Unicorn Realtors from time to time and I occasionally bring in a bank, but for the most part, this business is done buyer to seller, between people like you and me.

Why is it such a secret? Early in my career, I found out that the only people sharing creative finance methods liked to do so behind massive paywalls. They wanted you to pay $25,000 or $50,000 just to get the information. And, look, I paid a lot of those guys early on and only got bits and pieces of the information. That's one of the reasons why I give away so much information on social media. If you can start with no money down, why pay an arm and a leg to learn how?

But here's the other reason it's kept a secret. Schools don't really teach you what you need to know. They teach people how to be employees. Modern schools were set up during the industrial revolution to raise little workers. Unfortunately, they mostly still operate this way. Why didn't you learn to balance a checkbook in high school? Why didn't college teach you how to file your taxes? Why did no one teach you how to be a good spouse or parent? The most important lessons in life aren't taught in school. You have to learn them on your own, through proven paths, but also through mistakes and pitfalls.

I did 7,000 renovations and grew up with a dad who used creative finance, but it didn't seem plausible to me until Bethany and Eileen held my hand through the various steps. That's what I hope this book does for you. About 80 percent of what I do now is creative finance and it's made my life much easier, and I've helped thousands of people. Creative finance is just a way to buy anything. You can buy a house. You can buy a car. You don't need cash. You don't need credit. You don't need credentials.

But before we get too far into the book, I do want to address the elephant in the room. If you found this book after seeing one of my deal breakdowns on YouTube, know that some of those are particularly unique and not all deals are $0 down, zero percent interest. Yes, those deals happen, but they happen because you have come across hundreds of opportunities and have mastered negotiation. This isn't every single day, but that's the creative part. To use the baseball metaphor once again, you will strike out more than you get hits, and every season is made up of home runs, singles, doubles, triples, and groundouts. It's all part of the game.

The strategies in this book will work in every single state and in every single county, so they'll work for you too. Let's get started.

The Seven Layers of "Why?"

I'm going to sprinkle ideas about mindset through the book because it's vital to help you be consistent and take action. People think success in real estate is all about numbers, but, in reality, success also flows from your mindset. But there needs to be an underlying "why" to help fortify you and help you stick to your plan when it feels like the world is against you.

Have you done the seven layers of "why" test? It's a pretty simple test to help you determine what you truly want. The first layer is the surface layer. If your goal is to be a millionaire, your first question is likely "Why do I want to become a millionaire?" Your answer likely has something to do with supporting your family and finding financial freedom. You ask yourself "why" again. "Why is supporting my family and financial freedom important to me?" An answer has something to do with being content in life or maximizing your happiness. But it gets a little more difficult with each new layer. After you ask yourself "why" a few times, you have to dig deep to get an honest answer.

If you haven't already done the seven layers of "why," now would be a good time to put the book down, pull out a pen and paper, and go deep. The first question or two will be as obvious as the answers above, but you don't get to your real "why" until you go deep. This is the thing that will help you get up in the morning. This is the thing that will help you make calls when you don't feel like making calls. This is the thing that will truly help you make all the little decisions to change your life. This is the path to figuring out who you want to become. Take some time and dig in.

1. What do you want?
2. Why is that important to you?
3. Why is that important to you?
4. Why is that important to you?
5. Why is that important to you?
6. Why is that important to you?
7. Why is that important to you?

Now let's go deeper. You want to become a millionaire. Why? To provide for your family. Why? So they'll be set up for a great future. Why? So your children's children will be happy and have generational wealth. Why? Because you're fearful of what the future brings and you know you can be the one to change your path. Why? Because your purpose is to change the future for your children's children. Why? Because you never want someone you love to miss out on life.

Again, this is just an example, but knowing what you want, getting on the same page with your partner, structuring your day to pursue these goals, setting up accountability, defining your principles, and knowing your deeper fears is the key to your "why" representing who you can become with the right mindset. There's a great Michael Jordan quote about him not only wanting to be better than the previous day's version of himself, but better than what he believes he is capable of. Mindset is everything when you're trying to build something new and great.

Here's something I think about as an example of depth. Imagine a little girl's backpack. She's around 6 years old. She's in first grade. The backpack is pink and has some cartoon animals on it. Maybe there's a $50 price tag that hasn't been removed yet. That backpack is sitting on the front porch of a modest home early one morning. The school bus rolls up. The parents say goodbye to their little girl as she scoops up the bag and heads through the front yard to the road. When she gets on the bus, she has the biggest smile on her face, because she's showing off her new backpack to all of her friends on the bus.

But what we don't see is this: that same family in a store like Target where that little girl asked for a backpack. Her dad wants his little girl to have the things she needs for a better education, but when she asks, he has to look at his bank account on his phone. This is something he has to do nearly every day, if not multiple times per day. He tells his daughter, "Absolutely, sweetheart," even though he's hesitant because of the price tag. He doesn't show on his face that he barely has enough money in his account to cover groceries. When he checks his bank account, he has just under $100 in his checking account.

Now let's go back further. The father and mother, the night before, are going through their bills and the father just received his paycheck. After paying off all their bills, they see what's left to buy groceries. They have little money, but they do have enough to get by and he knows things won't always be this way, so they push on, making ends meet for another month. Let's go back further, to when the father picks up his paycheck from his job at the construction office. Then back to him working the job, where he's laying carpet on a Sunday afternoon, his wife and children helping him to save time and because this is the only time they get to spend together. He's got to work every single day to make ends meet, but he's able to do it.

How did he get this job in the first place? He just asked for some side work at a local construction company because his previous job laid him off. As this father asks for some side work, the owner of the company walks in, sees a man who just wants to work. The owner gives him a chance to come in and work. What we see next is all the pieces of the puzzle to make this happen come together. There's a homeowner who needs to sell their house to downsize and find a better property. There's a young family that needs to buy this house. There's a wholesaler scared to make their next call because they're unsure if they're going to be successful or not in this business. And here's the thing: This is everyone's story. This is your story. This is my story.

Someone needs you to be successful. Someone needs me to be successful. This is my purpose. This is your purpose.

What you do matters. What you do impacts so many people. This is a true story about a man I met while I was walking into the office to drop off a purchase contract. I saw him again the following Sunday laying carpet with his family on a job site. He told me the backpack story. Look, it may not be clear right now, but somebody out there needs you. The things you can do in this life are bigger than you. It's not about you. It's not about me. Right now, if you're new, you're likely blinded by the desire to simply feed your own family, but your commitment is more than that. You can't see all the other people you are able to help. All the future employees you can help put food on the table. All the kids you can help get through school and parents you can help retire. All the lives you can change. When you go deep enough, you can discover your "why." It's your responsibility to carry the torch forward and lead with vision.

CHAPTER 2

CREATIVE FINANCE
in Everyday Life

"Everyday women and men become legends."

—COMMON AND JOHN LEGEND, "GLORY"

You bought this book to learn about creative finance in real estate, but before we even get into the nuances of that, I want to explain creative finance in everyday life. Most people don't see it, but it's happening all around you. When you buy something with your credit card. When you make something you intend to sell. When you buy groceries. Even when you see a new hospital pop up in a busy city. Nothing is quite what it seems, and that's a good thing. You just haven't been profiting from it until now.

Take your time going through this chapter to learn the small lessons about creative finance in everyday life. They'll not only help you understand the different paths and nuances, but they'll also help you explain them to others when you're on a call with a seller and working out a mutually beneficial deal. Stories are key. Each story in this chapter is meant to be simple. If you skip ahead, you'll have all the ingredients you need, but you need to let them resonate. Like making bread, you have to allow time for the dough to rise.

This chapter is the foundation for things to come. Creative finance is all around you. You just don't know it yet. Learn these stories and feel free to make them your own. Some of my students tell these stories as "My friend Pace…" while others figure out another way to tell them using their own real-life examples. Either way, when you only have a few minutes to close a deal, you'll be able to close the deal on the phone or in person and walk away with a contract.

How Dad Bought Houses

Creative finance is a way to buy anything without credit, without credentials, and without cash. My parents had twelve kids and my dad was always self-employed. Because of his employment status, he couldn't buy a house in a traditional manner, so he figured out seller financing on his own. The problem was, he didn't use it for investment properties. He only used it to keep a roof over his family's head. Honestly, when I started my career, I followed the same path. I was too busy working to catch my breath and recalibrate everything I had learned. I bet a lot of you are in the same place. You're reactive rather than proactive. It's survival mode from an ancient time. But now, it's time to evolve.

We moved twenty-six times before I turned 19 years old. Every single time we moved, my dad bought a new house on seller financing or subject-to or lease option. Seller financing means he went to someone who already owned the house and bought it from them without having to get a bank involved at all. With subject-to, he did the same thing but the owner didn't own the house outright, so he took over payments on the mortgage and gave the owner some additional money. With a lease option, Dad would create a contract with the homeowner that stated he could either buy the property or move after a period of time. This way, he could lock in a lower rent rate and choose to buy or move later on. My dad used these methods twenty-six times but was too busy with daily work to see how he could use them to make money. I saw them twenty-six times but thought they were too complicated to scale, and I went on my own busy path that also blinded me for years.

This example is direct, but I bet you've been in a room with someone talking about a unique experience like this and you thought little of it. It's both common and not common all at the same time. People do it every day. Not just investors, but everyday people who have exhausted their options when it comes to following the system's normal pathway. When you get in a bind, you have to be creative. But think of all you can accomplish when you're creative from the start—when you're creative but also thinking about scalability.

My Mom's Craft Business

I had twelve siblings, so when the holidays came around or it was time for prom, Mom made everything by hand. She's an industrious woman; she made dolls for all of my sisters growing up. She made them purses when they started carrying money around. She made prom dresses when they got to high school. Like Dad, Mom started doing this out of necessity, but then she started to realize she could make a little extra money on the side. Before long, she got so good and so popular she had a waiting list for her products. Unfortunately, that didn't mean she had extra money for more supplies.

Mom would go to Michaels, that craft and hobby store, and check the price of materials. She had enough money to make things for her children, for the most part; everything extra went to groceries and rent and things like that. But Mom wanted to make more items and sell them, so she had to look into ways of getting store credit. Because neither of my parents had traditional employment, they didn't have high credit scores to reference or documents to confirm later payment. The store's requirements were simply too rigid for her to make them work. She had the demand, but she could not afford the supply.

Mom learned the store credit policy and found people from church to buy the materials for her. They used their credentials to open the lines of credit and then picked up whatever she needed for purses and prom dresses. Sometimes, these other people would just give her their credit card and let her buy whatever she needed. Then, after she finished making the dresses and purses, she would sell them for a profit.

On average, if she spent $1,000 on materials, she could make about $2,000 in return. With the profits from her materials and labor, she could then pay back the small loan and give the person who opened the line of credit a small kickback. They both benefited from this deal. My mom did this over and over. In a nutshell, these are examples of Airbnb arbitrage and subject-to. You can rent a property from someone with better credit and then sublet that property as an Airbnb. You can also take over a lease subject-to. As long as you make more money listing the property on Airbnb than you pay each month in rent or for the loan, you've got a profitable business. The same is true for basically any type of business. Buy low, sell high.

My Famous F-150 Story

I've told this story 1,000 times and I'll tell it 1,000 more because it's one of the simplest ways to understand creative finance. In fact, there's a longer version in Chapter 8 where I tell it to a seller. I'm including both because I want you to see what types of questions a seller asks when you break down the various elements of the story. When you tell this type of story to a seller, you answer why a seller would do this. You answer why a buyer would do this. You answer how it benefits both parties. You answer why creative finance is sometimes preferred over cash. Whenever a seller tells me, "I don't understand seller finance," this is my go-to story, and it's all thanks to my wife, Laura.

Back when I was a contractor, I had this Ford F-150 that I cherished but didn't need anymore. It had well over 300,000 miles on it but it ran like a champ. I checked the Kelley Blue Book and it said it was only worth $5,000 or so. This truck had done a lot of work for me and I knew, deep down, it was worth way more than $5,000 despite what this book said. I took a chance and listed it on Craigslist for $10,000.

Guess how many calls I got? That's right, zero. It was too much. No one cared what I thought about the truck and my personal interest. Everyone else in the world only cared what Kelley had to say about this truck. I was complaining to Laura about this and I told her I didn't want to list it for $5,000 because I knew the offers would be closer to $3,500 because that's just how it works on Craigslist. That's when Laura said something genius.

"Pace, you're the creative finance guy, why don't you just sell it creative finance?" A lightbulb went on. I had missed the obvious. I relisted the truck, but I made one small change. "F-150, Will Take Payments." Now I was flooded with offers. I had to take the ad down within forty-five minutes. Not everyone had an extra $10,000 lying around, but anyone with a job could make payments. All in all, I sold the truck for $12,500 because I gave someone the ability to make payments. The same is true when I buy houses today. If you're willing to take payments, I'm willing to pay more than anybody else. I tell this story to nearly every seller, agent, and title company I do business with because it simplifies seller finance and everyone immediately connects with the analogy. Some of the best deals I've ever gotten came from telling this exact story.

The Sub-To Car

I've sold a car on seller finance and I've bought a car subject-to. We call it the Sub-To Car and it's equally sentimental to my old F-150. My videographer asked if you really could buy anything subject-to. To prove my theory, we got on Craigslist and started reaching out to car owners who had their cars listed for sale. The F-150 was paid off, so that's how I was able to make payments, but when we looked at newer vehicles, they often still had leases or payment structures to the dealer attached. This is where subject-to comes in.

We reached out to ten people who had cars we liked, six responded, and we found one who was open to the idea. "I'll pay asking price if you let me take over the payments," I said on the phone. This is important. I said "take over payments" not "assume payments." This person was in a situation where they were open to the idea. The owner had recently been diagnosed with leukemia and could no longer afford the vehicle. But if he sold it straight up for cash, he wouldn't make anything on the deal.

We worked out a way for me to take over payments and then I'd also give him $1,000 cash to take the car. There wasn't equity in the car because it was only about two years old, so this was a better deal for this car owner than trying to sell for cash, where he would just be getting rid of the car or even losing money. I take pride in knowing we have a Sub-To Car that anyone can borrow when they come to visit our business. But, further still, we rent out this car on Turo, so while it costs about $400 per month, we also earn $2,000 a month from it, making about $1,600 a month in profits, to bring this deal full circle. Meanwhile, the car is still in the original owner's name and no one had to run my credit for this cash flow.

Every Time You Buy Groceries

Hopefully these previous stories resonate, but if you weren't looking for entrepreneurial ventures early in life, you may never have noticed similar stories happening around you. Let's talk about something we all do, every week. We all buy groceries. Most of us buy groceries with a credit card because we can rack up some points as we buy our everyday needs. You go to Costco or wherever you buy groceries and you get $200 worth of food for your family. You go through the check-out, swipe your credit card, and then take your bag and receipt. But if you're using a credit card, who owns the groceries—you or the lender?

This is a simple question I like to pose. With a credit card, you're technically using someone else's money to buy the groceries, but you've got them in your hands. Who owns them? One investor will say, "You do." Another will say, "The credit card company." Then someone will clarify, "You're holding them. They're in your hands." This is true and possession is important, but they've missed one key element: the receipt. It's important to hold the asset, but it's more important to have proof you hold the asset.

When you buy a house, it's the same thing. You use the bank's money but your name is on the deed. The deed is the receipt. And the deed and the mortgage are not the same thing. Ownership and debt are not the same thing. The bank has control of the mortgage but you have control of the deed. It's your house, even though you're paying the loan back to the bank. The deed is how you prove ownership.

When you leave Costco, they ask to see your receipt. They want to make sure you've transferred ownership from the store to your cart and the receipt is proof of transaction. They don't ask which credit card you used. That part is over. They don't care if you used your own money or someone else's money. They don't verify anything other than ownership. This receipt in real estate is called a deed.

Your Metaphorical Hot Dog Stand

Let's take the grocery example a step further. You bought the groceries, they checked your receipt, and now you're in the parking lot. You're about to load up your groceries when someone walks up to you and asks to buy everything in your cart. This guy says, "Hey, I saw you have literally everything I want and I don't have time to go into the store and I don't even have my wallet on me. Can I take your groceries and your receipt? I'll send you $200 and another $20 for your trouble if you are willing to take payments."

This is unlikely, but technically, you can do this. The store doesn't care. The credit card company doesn't care. This person doesn't have credit or cash or credentials (or even a Costco card), but they can work out an agreement with you and you can make more money on your purchase. And the reason they would offer you more is because they see extended value in the product beyond what you were planning to do with it.

Let's go just a bit further. Let's say you don't sell your groceries to this guy in the parking lot. Let's say you walk across the street to your hot dog stand. You take $200 worth of groceries and turn them into $500 in hot dogs and drinks. These are three different exit strategies based on one initial trip to the grocery store. Anyone can do this, but your exit strategy is going to be dependent on your business model. I generally look to cash-flow properties (that is, to make money each month from them), but I also do wholesale deals and everything else in between. We'll go into all that in just a few more pages.

My Friend Tyler's Business

Every entrepreneur has that one friend who has a family that feels like they've just made it. They have the big house. They always have plenty of extra food. They're giving to the community. They travel often and travel well. Honestly, this is the reason so many people connect with Robert Kiyosaki's book *Rich Dad, Poor Dad*. My friend Tyler had this family growing up. Even today, I think about how much that shaped my ambitions later in life.

Not long ago, Tyler's dad, Larry, passed away. Larry was the breadwinner for the family. He ran an insurance business for years and years, but had retired somewhat early. At Larry's funeral, I got to catch up with Tyler and his family. I asked them what Larry had been up to the last twenty years of his life and how he used his retirement. They told me some fun stories, then shared Larry's brilliant exit strategy.

Larry sold his insurance business to his kids on seller finance. He calculated what he needed and worked out a deal where they would give him $15,000 a month for the rest of his life. This way, they got the business and they also got to use Larry's reputation. They kept his name on the door so his regular customers wouldn't abandon ship and it worked out for everyone. They started making money off their father's empire while Dad went off into the passive income sunset to retire.

Larry was fortunate to have kids who wanted to run the business, but a lot of entrepreneurial parents aren't so lucky. But that doesn't mean this isn't an option both for the business owner and those looking to take over the business. From another perspective, you can take over an existing business with a piece of paper. You can buy a business that's been running strong for thirty years and start making money right away as you pay off the business. This sort of thing has been done for thousands of years. Most people just aren't aware it's happening all around them. That's creative finance. That's seller finance. And, obviously, the same is true for the housing market.

Creative Finance Is Everywhere

Most people are blind to creative finance, but it's everywhere. It's not just in small businesses, the grocery store, and hot dog stands. Big companies use it all the time. When you see an apartment building or a new hospital or a fancy hotel go up, none of these are being bought with cash. They're all being bought with some sort of creative finance; it's just not always clear to the public that this is how business works.

The same is true for your mortgage. Banks sell mortgages all the time on the secondary mortgage market. You receive a letter in the mail saying your loan has changed hands and now you're paying a new mortgage service to handle these payments. Banks, investors, and financial institutions trade mortgages, servicing rights, and mortgage-backed securities to either free up money or make more money. Most homeowners aren't aware of it, but the secondary market has a huge impact on how the primary market operates.

But that doesn't mean it's just for big shots. Everyone has the ability to make money with creative finance. I sold America's No. 1 vehicle on creative finance and it benefited everybody. The same is true for the Sub-To Car. You don't need a down payment. You don't need cash. You don't need a W-2, pay stubs, or tax returns. It's happening all around you and behind your back, so now it's time for you to get in on the action. Once we get the blinders of tradition off, we can start to see all of the opportunities around us.

Why isn't creative finance mainstream? In my opinion, it's because most people overcomplicate it. If you can't explain it to a third grader, you can't explain it at all. I'm going to break it down like that. I don't feel you're like a third grader, but, like I said earlier, you need to fully understand the nuances so you can explain them when the time comes. Read these stories over and over again. Use them or adapt them when you explain seller finance to other people. I wish someone had told me all this when I got started. It would have saved me a lot of time, energy, and money. These are real-world examples that will hopefully give you your own epiphanies of how you can build wealth as a creative problem solver. Every time I get a deal, it's because of a simple story like the ones listed here.

Let's talk creative finance in real estate.

CHAPTER 3

Why Do People Buy Real Estate?

"We can't do nothing about the past, but we can do something about the future that we have."

—LUPE FIASCO, "ALL BLACK EVERYTHING"

There are only five reasons people buy real estate: positive cash flow, depreciation, appreciation, mortgage paydown, and leverage. That's really it. Now, all five can help your business, but as your business grows, your motivation and portfolio may change. I'm a cash flow guy, personally, but I think about all five reasons whenever I'm considering a new property. They all help form your business and your overall portfolio.

Reason 1: Cash Flow

The first reason people buy real estate is cash flow. That's something I'm going to repeat over and over in this book. For me, cash flow is a major priority. I want to make sure there's more money coming in than going out each month. For some people, this is the only reason to buy real estate.

When looking into an investment property, cash flow comes down to income and expenses. Cash flow is the amount of profit you bring in each month after collecting all income, paying out all operating expenses, and setting aside any reserves for future repairs. For buy-and-hold investors, cash flow is crucial to increase their income. It allows people to invest in other properties, create a safety net with their expenses, or do anything they want with the excess money. I live off cash flow.

How do you calculate cash flow? A simple, overly basic method would just be to take gross rental income and subtract all expenses and cash reserves to find cash flow. For example, if your income is $1,000 but you pay out $350 for the mortgage, $200 for property taxes, $50 for insurance, $100 for property management, and then toss another $150 toward vacancy and repair reserves, you end up with only $150 in cash flow. That other $150 (vacancy and repair reserves) will sit in your war chest, but you have to assume it will be used eventually. Some people would take this deal, while others would not. More than likely, if you want a deal with only $150 per month in profit, you're thinking about more than just cash flow.

Some potential problems in this scenario would come from any unexpected increases in expenses from tenant turnover, missed rent, vacancies, property taxes, and insurance. At the same time, you can improve your cash flow over time with increased rent, good long-term tenants, preventative maintenance, and refinancing.

In the end, investing in real estate is all about the numbers. Cash flow is and will always be a major factor in how I do business. Wherever you are starting out, it's important to understand your own investing criteria and your goals.

Reason 2: Depreciation

The second reason people buy real estate is asset depreciation—tax benefits. I'm in the phase of my business now where when I look to buy properties, I think a lot about depreciation. Basically, depreciation is the tax benefit of how assets wear over time. To get a little more technical, depreciation refers to deductions in the value of real estate over the lifetime of a property. The Internal Revenue Service has specific rules and regulations in place to govern depreciation. This is really important when you think about your portfolio. Rental property owners use depreciation to deduct from the purchase price and improvement costs come tax season. Depreciation begins on a property as soon as the property is available to use as a rental. Investors can deduct the cost of buying and improving a rental property, but rather than taking a large deduction at the end of the first year, an investor can use depreciation across the life span of the property. Typically speaking, the IRS calculates most U.S. residential properties as depreciating around 3.636 percent each year for 27.5 years.

According to the IRS, a property is depreciable when you own the property (including through debt), when you use the property in your business as an income producer, when the property has a determinable useful life, and when the property is expected to last for more than one year. This doesn't apply to land or even landscaping; land can't be "used up" so it doesn't depreciate.

Generally speaking, to estimate depreciation, you have to determine the basis of the property. This is the cost to acquire the property, including any legal fees, recording fees, surveys, etc. Then you separate the cost of the land and buildings. Once this is done, you can start to determine the value of the house and make any needed adjustments. Wherever you're at in your business, look for experts to help you calculate these costs so you can keep more money in your pocket.

Reason 3: Appreciation

Third, real estate offers appreciation. This is when the value of the property goes up. For a property owner, an increased property value can lead to a profit upon future sale. In some ways, when you do a real estate deal, you're dealing with the future evaluation of the property just as much as—or even more than—the current valuation of the property. This isn't a guaranteed number, but it's something to track over time. That's why it's an investment.

Appreciation means you are keeping up with the market or improving the home even beyond normal, local standards. The average appreciation varies tremendously based on factors such as location, the housing market, and the property condition; currently (late 2022), the average home appreciation is 2 percent month to month or about 14.5 percent over a year, but some years you'd be lucky to see 4 percent year over year.

If your home is worth $200,000 when you purchase it and the market has increased in a way that the home is now worth $225,000, then you have $25,000 in appreciation (a 12.5 percent increase). The U.S. Federal Housing Finance Agency offers a calculator to help you better determine these numbers. You can also read the chapter on comping to determine the overall value based on the local neighborhood.

You can "force" appreciation by making improvements to a property that increase its value. Common numbers come from interior and exterior upgrades, increased energy efficiencies, and increased square footage, but there's so much you can do to increase the appreciation of a property. That said, unless you are looking to tap into the gained equity (such as through a refinance), this value really only matters when you plan to resell the property and cash out.

Reason 4: Mortgage Paydown

Fourth, there's mortgage paydown. In many cases, not only are investors earning cash flow, but rental income is actually paying down the mortgage of the property (meaning that, assuming the cash flow makes sense, investors are essentially getting the property for free).

Let's compare mortgage paydown to cash flow. If your goal is financial freedom, you're going to need deals that cash flow. But if your goal is to crowdsource your retirement, then cash flow is less significant in the beginning and you can have renters who simply pay down your mortgage while you break even—or close to it—for the first few years.

That said, even minimal cash should grow over time. Your goal is to focus on appreciation and raise rents with the market. If you cash flow $100 per month the first year, you should make $125 or so the following year, depending on your market, all the while paying off the mortgage. After a few decades, your cash flow will increase, and the mortgage will be paid off.

Once the mortgage is paid off, you no longer have that bill, meaning the cash flow will increase or you can sell the home and cash out the total amount. Again, it's all about your overall goals. I would advise having a variety of rental deals as your goals change.

Reason 5: Leverage

Fifth, there's leverage. When you buy real estate, you're building leverage for yourself and for your business. I call this the 50 Million Dollar Mindset. If you're serious about this business, it's not crazy to build assets worth $50 million. You just need to set up a scalable business using the processes in this book, and whatever number you want to build, you can build. That's leverage. High-level sellers will seller-finance me major projects because of the equity I already have. This means I don't have to technically refinance a property—I can use properties as collateral to acquire even more properties. That's leverage in a nutshell.

Finally, the bonus reason people buy properties is to tell stories. In some cases, that's why I buy specific properties—just to tell stories about how you can buy those types of properties. Build momentum, create stories, and focus on all these aspects as you build your business. If you're building a brand in the real estate niche on social media, which I highly recommend you do (as it will bring in more deals than you can imagine), you're going to need interesting stories to tell so people notice you, your business, and your skill sets.

INVESTOR STORY
Elena Tang—Sub-To Deals
"There's more to real estate investing than cash flow . . ."

Elena Tang says many of her highlights are lessons in what not to do. It's vital to teach what you have learned along the way. Deals don't always cash flow like you believe they will and there are always potential problems with any deal. Interest rates change. You might miscalculate deals. These things happen. Learn from someone slightly ahead of you and grow at your own pace. No matter where you come from, you can break the generational curse and change your life. Elena says, "My marketing is serving the community, because that's what I'm best at."

Elena has five deals that are only cash flowing about $1,000 per month, but there's so much more to the story. There's appreciation. There's depreciation. And there's so much more she has learned in this business and so much further she has to go. Cash flow is my main priority, but it's not my only priority and it's not the only way to make money.

Elena said that all five of these deals have helped other people. She considers herself to be a social worker who dabbles in real estate. When she heard me say that creative finance helps homeowners, she signed up for a workshop right away.

Her first deal was with a tired landlord with a duplex in Tampa, Florida. The landlord agreed to sub-to. The back unit had a nonperforming tenant; a friend of a friend of the landlord wasn't paying but the landlord also didn't want to kick him out. Elena's holding it as a long-term rental, where it cash flows about $400 per month.

The other four deals are also making something like $400–$600 per month, so after all of her expenses, she cash flows around $1,000 per month. For me, all of my best stories come in hindsight, so Elena, in her first year, hasn't been able to use depreciation. Each house cost around $30,000 down because they were all creative deals, but the Tampa property alone is valued at $285,000. This means she has around $1.25 million of real estate under her management. Sure, she's only cash flowing $1,000 right now, but the foundation is there for the future.

If you think about $1.25 million of real estate, you get back approximately $318,000 as a deduction (this is based on IRS tax depreciation data and not a guarantee). In reality, the property is not going to lose value, but this is how the IRS thinks about properties, assuming you'll do nothing to update it. People who make $100,000 per year pay more than I do in taxes each year. This should be taught in school, but it's not, so you have to figure it all out on your own. For the next 27.5 years, Elena can write off $45,000 per year for depreciation. That's the benefit of these types of deals even if you're not making what you want to make at first.

KEY TAKEAWAY | As long as you own real estate and work to grow and expand, you're getting more value than you think.

CHAPTER 4

Strategies to Purchase Properties

"Generational wealth, that's the key. / My parents ain't have sh**, so that shift started with me."

—JAY-Z, "LEGACY"

"I'll pay you $40,000 over the asking price," I said into the phone, on a live recording, during one of my regular sessions with several hundred of my students. "There's 40,000 more reasons this should work for you." It always takes a minute or two for this to register. It sounds too good to be true. I mean, why would anyone pay an extra $40,000 for a house? That's a luxury car. That's college tuition.

But here's why: It's a winning scenario for everyone involved. "You just blew my mind," I've heard one seller say. "I can't believe you'd be willing to do that," said another. I let this sink in as I continue to build trust over the phone.

"Would this number work for you?" I asked.

"This can work," said Susan, the seller I was speaking with that day with the class, as the wheels in her mind started to sync with mine. Over a handful of follow-up calls, we went over the numbers in more detail, wrote up the paperwork, and made the deal.

How does this work? Why pay $40,000 over asking price? I do deals like this all the time. In fact, I've closed hundreds of deals in a similar manner. I don't always pay more. It's not like I'm eager to overspend on every deal. I'm certainly happy to pay less, but I'm willing to pay more when the numbers work in our favor. This particular deal makes an excellent case study, so first I want to break down the numbers. Then I'll go over the details and mindset throughout the rest of the book. In this scenario, I worked out a deal that was $0 down, zero percent interest, and, for me, that made it the deal of a lifetime.

For this deal, I bought the house in the spring and set up a first payment due six months later. We structured the second payment twelve months after that. Susan agreed to pay the closing costs because she wanted to keep a tenant in the property for the remainder of his lease. The property didn't need a renovation, so there were no expenses to worry about there. Where most people worry about overall costs for the whole deal, I like to laser-focus on monthly costs. What comes in? What goes out? This is how you build wealth. This is how credit card companies work. This is how banks work. The payment structure we broke down was $375 per month paid to Susan with the magical interest of zero percent. The tenant whom Susan had set up for me was paying about $1,650 per month.

How do these numbers break down over a thirty-day period?

I bring in $1,650 per month from the renter.

Subtract $375 that goes to Susan.

Subtract another $275 for miscellaneous expenses like insurance and whatnot.

Then the property nets me a clean $1,000 per month.

That's profit. That's net. That's what I can put in my pocket just for structuring the deal correctly and taking on the "responsibility" of managing this location. In a nutshell, this is creative finance.

Let's go back to those initial payments that we structured out. I had one payment of $5,000 due six months in and another $5,000 paid twelve months after that. In this particular deal, the tenant paid my down payment and future tenants will pay off the entire house. If my team does nothing but manage the property for the next twenty years, this property will bring in another $240,000 while paying for itself (and this doesn't even adjust for inflation or natural rent increases year after year).

I'm not paying $40,000 more for a property. I'm investing in a future asset that will bring in close to $1 million when you factor in monthly profits and future equities. That's creative finance. It's a long-term strategy that brings in cash flow from day one. All you have to do is find sellers willing to see the long-term value with you. Are there objections? Of course. And not all sellers are in a position to do deals like this one, but your job isn't to convince someone incapable of understanding this to make a deal with you. Your job is to find those who are willing to come along for the ride. You control your future.

There are going to be roadblocks. There are going to be obstacles. But whether you're a complete newbie or a veteran closer, it's time to be relentless toward your vision and what you can build for yourself and your family.

Ideal Creative Finance Conditions

Everyone wants to know the ideal creative finance situation, but what you really need to know is the ideal creative finance situation for yourself and your business model. I like long-term deals for my portfolio, but I also use creative finance on short-term flips and wholesale deals. Everyone is different. What makes up your buy box? What problems can you live with? What headaches do you want to avoid? Some people I talk to only want to buy multifamily properties. Others want to work out of state. And some only want to work on deals within an hour of where they live. What I want to focus on is what makes your perfect deal. I'm going to give you a handful of options to choose from. There's subject-to. There's seller finance. There's a hybrid model. There's the Morby Method, which is something I created for creative deals where you borrow money back from the seller. There are novation agreements. There are lease options. There are executory contracts. Then there's arbitrage. All of these are tools for your kit. Let's talk about finding your perfect deal, the characteristics of a bad deal, and how to find a good deal in the first place.

I can't stress this enough: It's *your* perfect deal, not *the* perfect deal.

It's about your individual personality, what resonates with you, and what's important to you. There are key elements to focus on, but every investor has a different appetite. Imagine you go to a restaurant and there's a full menu. You can get a chicken sandwich. You can get a Greek salad. You can get a hearty steak. Knowing there's a full menu available gives you options to figure out what makes sense for your portfolio. You need to ask yourself what kind of investor you want to be.

For me, I want to be an investor who cash flows (in the Susan deal mentioned earlier, I was able to cash flow $1,000 from the first month). Beyond cash flow, about 80 percent of my deals are in Arizona, where I live, and the other 20 percent are in locations where I visit frequently and know I can find good deals.

As of the writing of this book, my buy box list includes Arizona, California, Colorado, Florida, Georgia, Idaho, Montana, Nevada, North Carolina, Tennessee, Texas, Utah, and Wyoming. For the most part, the similarities in these areas are that they are all warm areas (except for Utah and Wyoming, but I grew up in these locations and understand what makes up a good deal in each). When I say "warm," I am talking about literal temperature, not just hot areas to do business. You have to do deals in places where people are consistently moving to and consistently renovating properties. If it's freezing outside over half of the year, people are not renovating houses. It's physically too cold. In these out-of-state markets I only do creative finance deals, but here in my home state of Arizona I do a little bit of everything. This includes cash, creative finance, and the BRRRR method (buy, rehab, rent, refinance, and repeat).

For many new investors, I recommend finding their first property in their local market. This doesn't mean this should change your plans for your overall portfolio, but starting local—as close to your house as possible—allows for you to skip a few steps in the learning curve, because you already know certain things. Whether you've bought your first home or not, you probably know a few things about the area and it'll be easier to talk to the seller because you'll have that fact in common. I bought the majority of my first few properties in areas I could drive to easily, areas I understood, areas that were appreciating, and low-crime areas. This is true for the majority of people in real estate, whether they've done one deal or thousands of deals. Buying local lets you dip your toes in the water without feeling overwhelmed as you try to comp and line everything up to close a deal.

Aside from location, you should also consider whether you plan to manage the property yourself. If you're a handyman, this might be an option and will save you around 10 percent of your profit for regular repairs and upkeep, but you'll also be on call round the clock if any issues should arise at the property. Obviously, you can manage a property in the beginning and then find someone else to help later or vice versa, but it's really a question of time or money.

Personally, since I was a general contractor for over ten years, I was able to set up my own property management team; I didn't see it as a good call to give away 10 percent of our income in the beginning. Other investors I know would never want to deal with tenants and toilets. They don't want to fix things. They don't want to deal with people who are late on rent. Typical renters, after all, are known to complain, whereas lease option renters or wrap deals hardly ever complain because they have more of a pride of ownership (we'll go over these terms later in the book, and there's also a glossary of terms in the back). It depends on what type of business you want to build and what headaches you can live with.

Why Cash Flow Is a Priority

When I think about a sub-to deal (aka subject-to deal), I picture a hearty rib eye steak. In other words, cash flow is the primary element that makes up a good deal for me. There are sides, sure, but if that rib eye isn't cooked to perfection, the plate (or deal) is a bust. Some of these side benefits to the main course include location, type of house, neighborhood with low vacancies, and good schools, but cash flow is crucial. It's the North Star for me in terms of what makes or breaks a deal.

Let's talk about your first rib eye. When you find a deal within two hours of your house, you know you can drive by on a Saturday morning or stop by after work to visit the property and make sure things are running smoothly. Get out there and drive by the property. Pay attention to the neighborhood. Pay attention to the ebbs and flows of this environment. What are the pros? What are the cons? In addition to maintenance, there's also a pride of ownership. Every time you visit the property, you know that house is making you money every single month. It's appreciating. It's giving you tax benefits. There's nothing like being able to drive by these properties. I would focus on this type of deal for your first few properties.

To further elaborate on areas with low vacancies, you need to make sure you're not buying in a problem area. If you see an overwhelming number of vacancies compared to the population of the area, you could have a problem renting the property. There could be excessive crime. There could be businesses leaving at a higher-than-normal rate. There could be other red flags as well, so try to learn all you can about an area before you start doing business there.

What makes an area bad? Again, it's high crime, high vacancy, and low rent, but this doesn't mean I don't occasionally buy properties in "bad" areas. High crime is not necessarily a deal killer for me, but high vacancy and low rent are deal killers. For a lot of those high-crime areas, I just need to be more diligent in screening tenants. Use reliable programs to screen tenants and when you make rules for finding a tenant, don't break your rules. Stick with them. These are my goals and my flavor of rib eye, but I've got friends in the industry who like to pick up cheap houses in "bad" areas. They're willing to deal with the headache or perhaps they've got a great property manager who can deal with it for them. Again, you have to decide what works for you.

If you're not sure how to determine these factors, start by looking for a crime heat map. They're super easy to find online. As a long-tail keyword, look for "crime heat map" and then type in the county and/or state you're looking to do business in. Essentially, it'll look like a snow forecast. There will be shades of color with the darkest representing higher-crime areas. Categorically, it will also tell you what type of crime such as "theft under $500" or "theft from building," but using the map will help you target low-crime areas if crime is something you prefer to avoid. You want to have pride of ownership and things could change over time, but always look for the sweet spots and stick to criteria that work for your long-term portfolio.

What makes an area good? The basics for me are areas with low crime, low vacancy, nearby schools, nearby companies, nearby airports, nearby downtown areas, and sporting arenas. If you think about these various elements, you can find areas where larger corporations have already done the hard work for you. Think about companies like Trader Joe's, which are more spread out than, say, Walmart grocery stores. These companies are looking for population density as opposed to locations on every corner. The same is true for businesses like IKEA or Chick-fil-A. They're not everywhere. They're specifically somewhere. You should think of your deals in the same way. Do your due diligence on the factors that are most important to your deal. If you wouldn't want 1,000 versions of the same deal, then you shouldn't even do one version of it. It's not more complicated than that and most people get in trouble locking in deals that they wouldn't want to repeat.

Some of my best rentals are student rentals. Some people don't want the headache here, so it once again depends on how you want to work with property managers or deal with things yourself. I have a property that normally rents out for $1,800, but because I made it a student rental, I can rent it for $3,200. This way, a four-bedroom family home is turned into a four-person rental. I rent by the room rather than by the house itself. This works for college towns. This works for big company communities. This works for locations near airports. Some companies focus only on renting homes to airlines so pilots and other workers can stay there overnight rather than at a hotel. Some investors cater to traveling nurses. You can be an Airbnb company. You can be a corporate company. You can do whatever works for you. Just look for areas where you are more likely to have frequent renters and you can find your own sub-niche within a niche.

You also need to know what type of renter your property is going to attract. If you have a house in a college town and all the neighbors are college students, you're probably going to attract college students. I have some horse farms, which naturally attract a specific type of buyer. I quickly noticed that people who want land for horses and other conditions like that are willing to pay well over market rate for those properties. This doesn't always include excess land. These people were previously boarding their horses at another stable, so if they could rent from us, they could avoid those stable fees and have their animals nearby. I focused on horse properties for about three months once I learned this hyperspecific sub-niche. I have six properties that have a house and land nearby. Our best deal nets about $1,000 per month whereas the same deal without horses would only net us about $400 cash flow per month. This is a super-specific example, but find out when and why people are willing to overpay and cater to those people.

Structuring Creative Deals

In real estate, there are two ways to structure deals with sellers.

- **Option 1: Cash or Financing.** Most people know option 1. Either you have a bankroll to buy the property in cash (which is how you can offer less than a home is worth) or you seek out financing from a bank or other money lender. With this method, the seller gets paid in full and ownership is transferred to the buyer. It's best when the seller's situation is drastic and they need cash immediately or when the seller just wants to get out of the investment quickly for whatever reason.
- **Option 2: Creative Finance.** Here buyers can use an alternative way to acquire or control real estate without paying all or

some of the costs up front, like you would with cash or bank financing. As a real estate investor, it's important to understand both methods to close more deals. But, ultimately, the goal is to understand the situation the seller is in to know which method is best for any specific deal.

My friend Jerry Norton would tell you that this all starts with a two-step process. First, make a low all-cash offer, perhaps 60 percent of the value of the home, to see if the seller is in a position to sell for a discount. Remember the phrases "all-cash" and "close quickly" for this. Next, Jerry would tell you to counter with creative finance. In many cases, the seller will counter back with a higher price, whatever they see on Zillow. Counter back that you are willing to pay more if the seller will accept a creative finance solution. This way, you can find out what is most important to the seller: Do they want less money now or more money later? Generally, this depends on their situation. Did they inherit the house? Is there a divorce underway? Or do they have time to use creative finance, which will earn them more money overall? Let's talk creative finance methods.

METHOD 1: SELLER FINANCING

The first nontraditional or creative finance method is called seller financing or owner financing (or sometimes owner carry-back). Rather than the seller being paid in full, the seller agrees to sell the property with little to no money down and then carries the balance owed in the form of a seller-finance loan. Basically, the seller becomes the bank. When I speak to sellers, I like to say the seller graduates from a landlord to a lender. For example, if a seller agrees to sell you a property for $100,000, you avoid the bank or third-party financer, and instead set aside an amount of time in which to pay off the loan. Ownership would transfer like normal, but the seller would be the lender. This might mean paying the seller $2,500 per month for forty months. This method is great, as it can be a win-win for both parties, but it only works when the seller owns the property free and clear. If there's a mortgage, you have to use subject-to due to the debt in place.

METHOD 2: EXECUTORY CONTRACTS

The next method is to use what's called a land contract or contract of deed, depending on which state your deal is in, which is also an executory contract. This is similar to seller financing except you don't get the legal title of the property until after you've met the terms and paid off the full balance. As you make payments on the land contract, you will have what's called the equitable title to the property. This keeps the owner from selling the property to someone else or even putting the property on a lien. Like other creative finance methods, a land contract, under the right circumstances, creates a win-win scenario, so an investor can purchase the property with little to no money down. But, to protect your equitable title, file with your city or county a memorandum of land contract to put the public on notice of your interest in the property. Whichever method you use, always protect yourself and your business.

METHOD 3: LEASE OPTIONS

Then, there's the lease option, which is also known as the lease with the option to buy method. This is the most flexible method and easy to get out of for both the buyer and seller. A lease option is a contract between the owner and buyer that lets the buyer lease the property for a specified time with the option to purchase after that time, generally for a pre-agreed set price. The buyer or tenant has the option to buy but is under no obligation to do so. But the seller does not have the same exit strategy, meaning it binds the seller to sell if the buyer chooses to buy. This method is common in situations where the buyer wants to buy the property but is unable to qualify for traditional financing and may need time to save up more money or improve credit. Sometimes, to show good faith, the buyer puts down a nonrefundable option fee, such as 3–10 percent, which can be applied to the eventual purchase.

METHOD 4: SUBJECT-TO

A slightly more advanced creative finance method is called subject-to, or sub-to. The key here is to understand how real estate lending works. When someone buys a property and gets financing from an institution to pay for some or all of the property, that lender puts a mortgage or deed of trust lien on the property. This protects the lender because the owner has to pay off the lien in order to sell the property. Also, if there's a default, the lender can foreclose and take back the property. Sub-to is short for "subject to the existing financing." Rather than buying the property and paying off the existing loan, the investor takes over the existing loan payments that are already in place. The seller can walk from the property knowing the payments are being made, insurance is taken care of, and there are no additional hassles or further responsibilities to consider.

How to Structure a Subject-To Deal

Before we jump into details, here is a quick overview of structuring a subject-to deal.

1. First determine the existing loan terms.
2. Determine the equity.
3. Decide on your exit strategy.
4. Discover any out-of-pocket expenses that may play into the deal, such as overdue property taxes on the home.
5. Figure out if you need to put any cash in the seller's pocket.
6. Get an attorney or title company to wrap up the paperwork.

When structuring a subject-to deal, you first need to determine the existing loan terms. This includes the principal balance, the interest rate, the monthly payment amount, and whether there is a balloon or early due date to pay off the loan. To find out, simply ask the homeowner to provide the most recent mortgage statement or have them get a payoff letter from the lender. Lenders can easily email over a payoff letter.

Then you need to determine the equity. This means you need to figure out how much the previous owner owes based on what the property is worth. If their current balance due is $75,000 and the value of the home is $100,000, then there is a 25 percent equity, or $25,000 worth of equity, in the property.

After you determine equity, you need to figure out your exit strategy (see Chapter 6). If there is enough equity to make the deal work, you still need an exit strategy. You can either flip the deal or you can keep it as a long-term rental. Some investors like to hold if there is little to no equity but they still want cash flow. If, for example, the loan balance is $100,000 and the as-is value is also $100,000, then there's no equity. But if the interest rate is low and the total monthly payment is $500 but you can rent for $800, a buy and hold method will earn money as you build equity. Also, factor in any out-of-pocket expenses that may play into the deal, such as overdue property taxes on the home.

Then, during the negotiation phase, figure out if you need to put any cash in the seller's pocket. It's possible that you will need to give some cash to the seller at closing. This depends on the situation. If the seller views the home as a headache, simply getting rid of it will be enough. But, if you need to sweeten the deal or if they need money for whatever situation, deals can go smoother when you hand over some cash. Check your exit numbers to see what is possible. Consider $5,000–$10,000 for this, but it can certainly be more depending on any specific situation the seller is in and what you're willing to do to close the deal.

Finally, get an attorney or title company to wrap up the paperwork. Since not everyone is familiar with sub-to deals, it's a good idea to find an attorney to do the paperwork. A specialized expert will cost around $500–$1,000, but it's well worth the price to make sure it's done right. As I've said in other parts of the book, look for referrals by asking people who are currently in the real estate investment business in your area, specifically those familiar with creative finance.

INVESTOR STORY
Ingryd Hernandez—The Morby Method
"I would never work with that lender again . . ."

Ingryd Hernandez is a deal underwriter. In one of her more unique deals, she applied the Morby Method. Most of her business focuses on Joint Venture deals, which means other people bring her deals and opportunities when they need help crossing the finish line. Another investor brought her a deal from the MLS.

The seller wanted to sell off the property, but they wanted a two-year leaseback. With this type of post, they're really looking for an investor. The seller was in dire straits. They had a bankruptcy and some other legal issues. The court ordered that their free-and-clear property be sold off to pay off debts, including a $170,000 tax lien and about $90,000 in lawyer fees (at the time, they thought these lawyer fees were much less).

As an underwriter, Ingryd would tell you that sellers don't know their numbers. Often, they don't even know their house payment amount, the interest, or the bank they owe money to. When the seller said they owed some money to lawyers, they had no idea it was $90,000. With this in mind, Ingryd often works with title officers and makes sure she gets all the numbers right.

It took about two months to close the deal. The seller's initial representative said no to the first offer, but then they realized they needed an investor to make it work out. This was a five-bedroom home in Phoenix. A comp would say it was worth $600,000, but the seller wouldn't make nearly enough to move to another property. These are also known as penalty box sellers due to the bankruptcy, because they're unable to go out and simply get another loan. Their circumstances are limited.

If they had closed on the first deal, it would have worked out better for everyone. But, thanks to the seller's lawyer, they changed the language of the initial offer, and because they lost a month of time (due to dual agency) and created other headaches. Ingryd's husband, a Realtor, represented Ingryd and they made another $15,000, but that wasn't the initial goal for the deal.

The first offer was $510,000 Morby Method, which meant they were going to bring in a percentage as a down payment (20 percent down of 80 percent from a well-known lender) and the seller was going to carry the other portion (20 percent). Normally, you get the 20 percent down payment money from a private money lender, but you can also self-fund it. Ingryd had to self-fund it in this case because she was working with a well-known big bank and that was their policy.

In addition to the Morby Method, Ingryd set up a lease option as her exit strategy. The seller became the lease option tenant. The lease option was a $15,000 cost and the down payment was $127,500. Ingryd also got 2 percent of closing costs and the wholesale fee, which was $10,000 to the lead generator. In the end, if Ingryd didn't feel a personal connection with the seller, she likely would have walked away from the deal. That's how complicated the lender and the attorneys made it, despite everything Ingryd did to make it work. Ingryd said of the deal and her connection to the seller, "If it wasn't me, I don't think anyone else would have stuck it out." She's listing the property back to the original owner at $575,000 so they get a three-year lease option and can buy their house back.

KEY TAKEAWAY | There's a reason we choose to be creative, but when you bring in traditional models (like this bad well-known lender), you can still take a hit.

CHAPTER 5

Why Are Sellers Open to *CREATIVE FINANCE?*

"Money trees is the perfect place for shade."

—KENDRICK LAMAR, "MONEY TREES"

There are only a few reasons why people won't sell on terms.

But first, I want to talk about Marvin. Marvin lives near Virginia Beach. He plays golf. His wife was a middle school teacher for over twenty years. Marvin's wife has Alzheimer's and he just found out. He needs to unload a property and he's open to terms, but he needs a better explanation of seller financing. After one of my YouTube followers, Matt, set up a call, I got on the phone with Marvin to discuss his deal and see if seller financing was a fit for his property.

"Hi, Marvin, this is Pace. I'm partners with Matt. How are you doing? I believe you were expecting my call today?" After the initial pleasantries, I told Marvin I only needed a few minutes of his time.

"Matt said you were interested in selling the house and may be open to seller finance as a possibility?"

"What does that mean?" Marvin asked.

"It means you become the bank, and we pay the number you're looking for over time."

Since this was new to Marvin, he responded, "I don't think I'm interested in that at this time." I checked over my notes and got back to the call.

"The property is rented at the moment or vacant?" I asked. He confirmed the house had tenants renting at the time of the call. "I don't have a lease," he added.

"Okay, so the tenants are there month-to-month?"

He responded, "Sixty days."

"Okay, so they have to give you a sixty-day notice before they even get out?"

"I have to give them sixty days' notice. And they have to give me sixty days' notice," he said.

"So in a perfect world, what would you do with the property?"

"Sell it."

"Okay, and at what price?" I asked.

"For some reason, the city subtracted a bedroom. I got a master suite. And it turns out I've been on a couple of those websites and they say it was selling for $270,000. I don't think I'll get that, but we did spend $30,000 on the master suite."

"Got it," I told him. "The city is missing a room that's in there so their total room count is off. You're not getting as much value as you'd hope?"

"They said I'd have to get someone to come out and look at it and change the tax records, because the Realtors won't change it unless the city records show it has four bedrooms. I never heard of such—"

I politely interrupted, "Yeah, we deal with it all the time. We buy people's houses that have a little addition on the back, and because the thing wasn't permitted properly, other people might not want it. It might be perfectly fine structurally, but it's not considered permanent."

He said, "I don't know how it didn't get recorded. I had a few people who probably just didn't submit the paperwork. That's all it probably comes down to—something really simple. But I had a stroke during the renovation. And the guy had a stroke during the time he was building it and his son finished the work, so I don't know what happened."

"That might have been the hiccup. How long ago was that?" I asked him.

"Oh god, that was 2009 or so. I think it's been about ten years."

I reframed the question based on the additional information: "Okay, so what do you think you could get for the house in the situation it's in right now?"

"I think I'd be happy with $240,000."

"Right. If you got $240,000 on the market and then paid out commissions and all that stuff, you'd end up with $210,000 or so when you walk away."

"No, I don't want to get less than $230,000 even with commissions," he clarified, also revealing he hadn't considered Realtor fees and those other market penalties.

Determining Walkaway Money

"Okay," I said. "I'm not a real estate agent nor would I ever be a real estate agent. I don't want to get you confused. I'm not suggesting you pay me commission if I buy it. I'm just suggesting if you do sell it on the market, you've got to sell it for a price that you know is high enough that you would net $230,000. You would have to sell it for like $270,000 on the market, then pay commissions. And then you'd walk away with $230,000 to $245,000—somewhere in that ballpark."

"They want a charge," he said.

"Yes, 6 percent plus another 3 percent with closing costs, home warranties, inspections, all that. You're around 9 percent total. I think the national average right now is 11 percent to sell a house. If you listed it for $270,000 it sounds like that might be a hard stretch to get because you're missing that bedroom you mentioned. And you've got tenants in the house. That might be hard to sell too, but you could probably sell it for $250,000."

After a pause, he said, "Really? Right, yeah, probably $250,000 or $249,000 or something."

I continued. "Okay, if you list it for $249,000, what do you think you'd get in your pocket after commissions, closing costs, inspections, maybe doing the permitting, and so on?"

"I haven't really gotten to that detail."

"Can I tell you why I'm calling? Because I don't think selling it for cash is the way you should go. But you don't know me from Adam. Taking advice from me is whatever, but my thought is: If you want the highest you're going to get, selling it on the market is a headache and leads to $220,000 to $225,000 in your pocket. Why not sell it on seller finance at $270,000?"

"I don't know what I'm getting into with that," he said honestly. "I haven't looked at owner financing or seller financing."

"It's pretty simple. Do you have a loan? Or do you own it free and clear?"

"Yes," he said. "Own it."

"And how much are you collecting in rent right now?"

"$1,550 per month."

"Okay. And then out of that $1,550 you pay taxes, insurance, you pay all those things, you end up netting around $1,100, right?

"So what if we came in and gave you a monthly payment, and you acted as if you were the bank? And we settled on a number of, let's say, $270,000. And I started making you monthly payments on it. And you become the bank and I'm the borrower, except my payments are going to you and not some bank."

"Okay, but why do you want to do that?"

"Because we buy a lot of real estate. And the fastest way to buy real estate is to avoid going through banks and going through the application process. If I go to the bank to get a loan on your house right now, what am I going to run into? The bank is going to say, 'Hey, there's a nonpermanent addition here and everything else.' I'd have to deal with the same stuff you're dealing with in order for me to buy that house with the loan. Why would I go get a loan and have to come in and lowball you when I could come in and give you the number you're looking for?"

He agreed.

The Bank of Marvin

I continued, "And in that situation, it's a win-win, because I can avoid going through the banks. And I can avoid having to go through the permit. Everybody wins. At the end of the day, if I buy that house from you, I gotta go through permitting to get that extra bedroom accounted for. But if I go to the bank of Marvin, I say, 'Hey, Marvin, let's create a promissory agreement that says I owe you $270,000.' I give you a down payment so you have some cash in your pocket, and then I make you a monthly payment. I take over the headache of the tenant, I take over the headache of the insurance, and you just collect a monthly check without a headache."

"What kind of down payment are you talking about?" he asked.

"When I go into a bank like Bank of America or Wells Fargo or Chase, I always ask them, 'What kind of loan programs do you guys have?' And they tell me, 'We have loan programs at 3.5 percent down payment, we have 10 percent down payment, and we have 20 percent down payment,' and usually the bank is who tells me what they want. At the end of the day, you just tell me what you want and what you're comfortable with."

"And what do you do with the house when you get it?" he asked.

"We can do a variety of things. Sometimes we turn houses into assisted living homes. Sometimes we turn them into behavioral health facilities and we help people in bad situations. Sometimes we turn them into affordable housing. But ultimately, it's usually some sort of charitable thing where we're trying to help out people, and we get the government involved to help us out with all that kind of stuff as well."

Marvin thought it over, likely also thinking about the predicament he and his wife were in.

"It sounds like we're not going to make a decision on this call," I said. "Let me plant a couple seeds. And we could do a follow-up call. At the end of the day, here's the reason why people turn to seller finance. Number one, when you go and you sell it on the market, I don't care what you list it for—$249,000 or $259,000, whatever. That's not what you're going to put in your pocket. Right?"

"Right."

"You're gonna walk away with an unknown number. You're essentially crossing your fingers and hoping that you get as high as you can, because you're waiting for a buyer, and you're waiting for an agent to do their job. And then you have to pay an agent to sell your house. And you walk out with $220,000, then when you get that $220,000, what are you going to do with it? Are you going to go buy a Maserati?"

"No." He laughed.

"You save it. You don't have a return on it, it's just sitting in your bank account doing basically nothing at 0.5 percent interest or whatever. And with the way inflation is going, you're actually losing money. Most of the sellers who are selling to us on seller finance, they say, 'Look, I don't want to go through any of that headache. I just want the price I want,' which, for you, it sounds like $270,000 is the magic number. Let's say that we've come up with the magic number. And instead of just selling it to me on payments, you can charge me interest. Now your investment is making you more money than $270,000 over time. Does that make sense?"

"Yeah, it does," he said. "What's the interest rate at now?"

"Usually it's about 2.5 to 3.5 percent interest with banks right now."

"What about people who don't have good credit, what are they at?"

"They're 4.5 percent or more. Or they just get denied."

"How much down payment are people putting up on a house for $250,000?"

I answered, "At $250,000, with the loan programs that we're seeing, there are a lot of down payment assistance plans where the government's coming in and paying for their down payments. And then there's another one that's a 3.5 percent down payment program. And then the one that we see kind of rarely, but it still is around, is about 10 percent. Our business model is trying to help people who are going through assisted living, people who may be experiencing memory issues, or people who have physical disabilities, those types of things." I said, thinking about some other sellers I have worked with in similar positions to Marvin's.

"Okay," he said.

"I think with you, at the end of the day, it comes down to: Do you want a higher price? And do you want to squeeze out all your profits from this house? Or, do you just want all this money sitting in your bank account doing nothing? Most of my sellers who are selling on seller finance are sitting there saying, 'Man, I'm glad my money's not sitting here doing nothing.' Because if I gave you a check for $220,000 today, what are you going to do with it? That's the thing: If you sell or finance to me, you are investing. You are a note holder in real estate. It's the greatest investment of all time."

"Okay, that makes sense."

"Here's what I would want to do. It sounds like your magic number is $270,000. Then I'd like you to figure out what down payment and what interest rate you'd like and then let's have a follow-up call sometime next week. You want to do some homework for me and then we can touch base and have another conversation?"

"I'll do that. Thank you," he said.

Turn a No into a Yes

This is how you can take a no to a yes. We closed this deal on a later call and have hundreds more like this one on record (you can even find five free calls in my interview on *The BiggerPockets Podcast* episode 527, "300 Doors, 100% Creative Financing"). The key is to explain the situation in a way that makes seller financing a no-brainer for both parties. Marvin was apprehensive at first, but only because this isn't a traditional way to do business. If you look back over this dialogue, you will even notice the fact that I just ignored his first objection. He said he wasn't interested, but again, he said this because he didn't have enough information. He didn't understand that I was willing to put $50,000 more in his pocket than anyone else. When you're only familiar with traditional financing, this sounds insane. If nothing else, it gets their attention.

When a seller says, "I'm not interested. No, I'm not interested in that," I don't say, "Well, why not?" What I do is ask, "How much money can you have in your pocket? What do you need to walk away with?" And then there are a bunch of little things that I do there that so many people won't notice. But when Marvin said, "I want $240,000 at the end of the day," I knew he meant $240,000 in his pocket. I knew that's what he meant, but I needed for him to see the problem with this logic, so I took him on that journey. I said, "Okay, you sell it for $240,000, so you're walking away with $220,000 in your pocket." And then he came back: "Oh, well, I don't want anything less than $230,000." Now I've got him working himself down. We went from $270,000 to $230,000 real quick. That's my form of anchoring. You're introducing someone to a new world, so you have to explain the rules of that world in terms they are going to understand.

Then you search for the pain point. What pain did I find with Marvin that I kept hitting on? I found multiple pain points.

- He's got an unpermitted addition.
- He's not making that much money from the home.
- He's been dealing with tenants for years.

And so Marvin's thinking, "Man, this really isn't that great of an investment." And I got him to say that out loud. Once I got him there, I started telling him third-party stories about my other sellers selling, because I knew he wasn't interested in seller finance, but it all came down to making sure he understood what he would get. By having him back into the number, he did this for me. I just needed to guide him. How can I get this guy to back into the not-so-great number that he would get on a cash deal?

An old adage goes, "A man convinced against his will is of the same opinion still." It's one of my favorite quotes and I see this time and time again in seller calls. Me trying to argue this guy down and saying, "Honestly, I'm sorry, your other investor isn't going to pay $270,000 on a deal like this. You're asking too much money."—that doesn't get me to the end goal. There's no point in arguing with someone when you can simply take them on a journey.

You see how I chose my sniper bullets, right? I focused on Marvin's problems and simply guided him over to my side of thinking. It's better for both of us. He just needed to understand what he stood to gain and what he stood to lose. In these situations, you're not arguing with someone who is hell-bent on making a deal in the traditional manner. You're talking to someone who doesn't even know there's another way or a better way to do business. Everybody else is out there with a horse and buggy when you show up in the first Ford Model A. There are going to be some questions, but you can be the one to answer them and close the deal.

INVESTOR STORY
Daniel Nissim—Seller Finance Case Study
"I don't have credit in the U.S."

Daniel Nissim, originally from Tel Aviv, currently lives in the Pittsburgh area. He found the sub-to community after joining the TTP Pre-Foreclosure Mastery class, where we discussed talking to sellers in foreclosure. Previously, he was in the Israeli Air Force, where he worked as an air traffic controller. These days, his focus is real estate investment. Since he wasn't born in the United States, he doesn't have traditional credit and relies on creative finance (foreign-born investors can build up credit, but they generally have to start from scratch).

Daniel worked tirelessly to master English, his second language, and then real estate investing. He didn't have the money to hire a cold caller, but he learned how to pull a list of unlisted leads and got to work calling his first set of tired landlords himself.

One particular landlord told Daniel, "Stop calling me—I already sold the house." But Daniel persisted; the contract was there but the transaction wasn't sold. The landlord listed the property as FSBO (for sale by owner) and an out-of-state buyer made an offer. Despite telling Daniel not to call again and despite saying the house was sold, Daniel continued to follow up anyway, knowing that sometimes these deals fall through.

The deal did fall through. Daniel called about a day before

closing date and the out-of-state buyer did decide to walk away from the deal. With the buyer gone, Daniel was the front-runner to make a new offer, plus the tired landlord had gone through this new ordeal and had even more reason to want to sell.

When Daniel called, he learned of the cancellation and what the type of deal was. There was a tenant in the house paying $950 per month and the house was listed for $100,000. All of the cash offers were around $65,000 and the seller wanted to get $100,000. Daniel asked, "What if I can come up to your number—would you give me terms?"

At this point, the seller asked what he meant by terms (which is *always* the case). Here I usually teach people to tell their own version of the F-150 story that we described in the first chapter. And that's exactly what Daniel did. "I have this friend Pace and he sold his truck this way . . . ." The seller understood the idea of getting payments over time and closed the deal.

They worked out a free-and-clear seller finance deal. Daniel offered to pay $10,000 up front and then pay $250 per month for the house. This way, he could pay $10,000 and then spread out the other $90,000 across monthly payments. Daniel wanted thirty years, but the seller knew he wanted to retire in twenty years, so he agreed to $10,000 down, $250 per month, and then a balloon payment or cash-out at the end of the twenty-year point. This was also an interest-free loan, which is unheard of in traditional real estate.

Where do tired landlords come from? A lot of people are able to get five to twenty properties over the course of their investing career, but they aren't able to scale. They try to manage everything themselves and end up getting tired of dealing with tenants and toilets. You have to learn how to scale, factor in management fees, and learn to grow a business, not just a side hustle. It's worth a management fee not to fall into this trap.

KEY TAKEAWAY | The deal is not done until the deal is done. Follow up, follow up, follow up. About 20–30 percent of deals fall through. You can be there to close when no one else can.

CHAPTER 6

Exit Strategies to Make Money

"My mind on my money and my money on my mind."

—SNOOP DOGG, "GIN AND JUICE"

You've negotiated a deal and now you want your first check. How does this happen? What are your exit strategies? How do you dispo (disposition) the deal? How can you make money where you're not overcapitalized?

The No. 1 way I teach people to make money in this business is to be a wholesaler to either a homestead buyer or a cash buyer using one of the buying strategies. (A wholesaler is someone who obtains a contract on a property with the seller and then sells that property to an investor.) A homestead buyer is a family that plans to move into the property. This is not an investor, but an actual family that wants to live in the property. A cash buyer is an investor who uses their own dispo strategy (dispo meaning how they unload the property or make money on the deal) to close the deal. With wholesaling, you can take a fee from:

- A subject-to deal.

- A seller finance deal.
- A wrap.
- A lease option.
- A novation agreement.
- A note.
- An agreement for sale.

This is how you can quickly make, on average, $5,000–$40,000 and beyond with a wholesale deal. When done efficiently, wholesale deals can require little money out of your pocket. You're finding the deal and earning an assignment fee for the deal. Your job is to connect the seller to a buyer. Most wholesalers build lists and build relationships, so they end up working with the same people over and over again as they bring in new leads.

The flow of a wholesale deal is much simpler than the flow of a retail deal. Like any good investor lead, it starts by reaching out to a seller. You can do this by door knocking, texting, cold-calling, direct mail, and any other strategy that works for you, but we've covered that, so let's talk about the transaction.

Once the wholesaler closes the deal with the seller, they need to set up a purchase contract, which is basically instructions for the title company. Within that purchase contract, there should be text that confirms it is assignable. Now the wholesaler can assign that contract to another buyer. The wholesaler solves the seller's problem—possibly helping with a foreclosure or whatever reason they're willing to sell the house—and negotiates a deal that they can resell for more money. The assignment is how they make money.

In Phoenix, I've used KeyGlee for the disposition on countless deals. As an example, let's say I call KeyGlee and tell them I have a purchase contract of $200,000. I'd like to sell that contract for $215,000, so I then make about $15,000 on the deal. If they agree, I send them an assignment contract and then send both contracts to the title company. Now KeyGlee takes that new contract and heads out to find a cash buyer, a flipper, or even a homeowner. In turn, KeyGlee will make another $5,000–$7,000 on that transaction. In these situations, they do the work that I don't want to do, but you can also do this yourself. Again, this depends on scalability and how much work you want to put into the deal. In the end, there are multiple contracts and everyone gets paid on the deal. If you would like to educate yourself more, wholesaling is the worst-kept secret in real estate investing, so there is already a multitude of books, YouTube videos, and other online content on this topic.

Where do you fit into this puzzle? You can be a lead generator who finds the deal. You can be a middleman who connects wholesalers to flippers. You can be the end buyer. If you're the end buyer, you need to know how to raise private money, get a hard money loan, or use cash. However the money is brought in, the buyer connects with the title company to confirm escrow. Then the cash buyer needs to choose their exit strategy for the property.

In later chapters, I talk about strategy, scalability, and creating a portfolio, but here I want to include that I might wholesale a good deal just because it doesn't fit into my long-term buy box for my overall portfolio. This is true for any type of deal as I believe strategy is everything, and my strategy is to achieve cash flow based on certain parameters.

Wrap Exit Strategies

"Seller on a wrap" is an amazing way to get into the business with no money out of your own pocket. If you can take a property subject-to or seller finance or a hybrid model or an agreement for sale, you can sell those as a wrap. However, you can't use a wrap for a lease option or a novation agreement or a note, because you don't own the property. You can only wrap a deal when you own the deal. Let's use an example to explain wraps and how they can be used as an exit strategy.

You find a seller who agrees to a $210,000 purchase price. He wants a $5,000 down payment and the rest to be paid over thirty years with 3 percent interest. You step in with a purchase agreement that reiterates this information and allows for you to assign the property to someone else. That someone else is the buyer.

Your purchase agreement should give you thirty to ninety days to find a buyer, assuming you are in a position where you can't maintain the property or don't want that hassle for this particular deal. I call this wrap buyer a "penalty box buyer." The penalty box buyer is often someone who can't apply for a normal loan (about 40 percent of people get denied for a mortgage), or they're an investor who is using tax structures to limit their taxes. This buyer will purchase the property, in this example, for $265,000 with a $20,000 down payment at 6.5–9 percent interest rate for forty years. To clarify, you're wrapping the initial terms with your own terms. It's the same as getting a gift, rewrapping it, and regifting it to someone else. You cover their terms with your terms and make money on the difference.

The best part about this type of deal is that you can make money in three different ways. You make money right away, because you make $15,000 from the buyer's down payment as they're paying you $20,000 and you're only paying $5,000. The second way you make money is by financing the property. Then you make money on higher interest rates.

The seller's interest rate is 3 percent, but the buyer's interest rate is 6.5–9 percent. After the down payments, the buyer owes you $245,000, and you owe the seller $205,000, so you made $40,000 in equity on the home.

Here's the best part: You still make monthly cash flow even though you no longer own the property. All this money goes through the servicing company, so you also don't have to manage any of this. The buyer is paying the servicing company and the servicing company is paying both you and the original seller.

But here's my favorite part of a wrap deal when compared to a typical rental: If something breaks, you're not the owner or the landlord. You're a lender. You don't get involved. All you need to do is collect checks from the servicing company. You make money in up-front costs, as a monthly percent, and with built-in equity all for setting up the deal.

Lease Option Exit Strategies

One of my primary selling methods is lease options. Personally, I like this path because I still own the property after the deal has been made. I have a property on Gold Lane that I bought for $150,000 with a $5,000 down payment. The interest is 3 percent and the principal, interest, taxes, and insurance (PITI) is around $837 per month. The entry fee was another $10,000 in cash. There were no arrears for this, so this was just cash to the seller, some maintenance, minor repairs, and about $500 in marketing to find a buyer. To get this cash down payment, you can:

- Use your own money.
- Raise private money.
- Find a lease option fee (which is what we did in this case).

For this overall deal to work, I'm taking over a $145,000 mortgage as a seller finance subject-to deal. What do I do with this hybrid deal to make money? I went out and found a lease option tenant buyer. I used Facebook Marketplace and some bandit signs (cheap, handwritten signs placed around town) to find a buyer. They agreed to pay $185,000 (I take the after-repair value (ARV) of $165,000 and then estimate the appreciation value over five years) for the property with an option fee of $10,000, a lease payment of $1,350, plus a five-year option to buy.

At this point, we've got two contracts in place.

1. A contract with the initial seller
2. A contract with the new buyer

The buyer is leasing the property for an extended period of time, in this case, five years. Why would anyone want to do this when they can either buy or rent? Typically, a lease option has a higher payment than a rental, so why would they pay more for the opportunity to own it at some point? Here's why: The tenant has most likely been paying rent for some time and they've moved due to any number of reasons: community, work, their kid's school, and so on.

If they rent in an area, they know the rent will be raised the following year. The tenant isn't kicked out, but now they have to pay more money. But if they have a lease option, they lock in that rate even though it's more expensive the first year. The lease option tenant buyer is interested because they have an option to buy, but also because they're investing in the likelihood that the property rent rate will increase over time. From their perspective, they can save some money and they have the option to buy after five years. Again, this falls back on situations. Maybe the buyer has moved for work or for college and their circumstances are still unstable, but they don't want to risk paying higher rent rates or feel forced to move annually. From my perspective, they pay me $1,350 per month, but I only have to pay $837 per month. I've got positive cash flow of $513 per month. Plus, I have ownership of the property, and I get those tax benefits for the property.

Here are some questions you will get when working out this type of agreement.

- Does that $10,000 get refunded if they choose not to buy? No.
- Will that $10,000 go toward the overall purchase price? No. It's only meant to secure the option to buy.
- Do the payments of $1,350 go toward the purchase price? No, because these are two separate deals. They can buy the house at $185,000, but they're paying rent to me during this five-year period. From their perspective, I can't do anything with the property as long as the lease is in effect. This might not sound like a good deal for the tenant buyer, but they're locking in a rate that could otherwise change over time due to appreciation in the area. It depends on their perspective and their situation for a deal like this to work out for both parties.

Personally, I now raise private money for those entry fee amounts, because relying on the buyer to pay the option fee adds some extra stress to finding a buyer in a short time period. When you start to scale, you can focus on smoothing out some of these wrinkles, but again, there are three ways to raise that initial money, so you can choose the method that works best for you.

Like any of my exit strategies, my overall goal is cash flow, but you need to decide what works best for you, the seller, and the buyer when you're making these types of deals. Solve problems. Create value. Try to be fair with everybody, and look for situations where everybody walks away content with the deal.

Sub-Tail Exit Strategies and Novation Agreements

What is sub-tail? (I coined this phrase, so if you see people outside of my circle talking about this, know it started with our team in Arizona.) Anyway, let's talk about "subject-to-retail." You get to own the property temporarily, then flip it on the retail market. With this exit strategy, you're going to see a lot of novation agreements, which is the process where the original contract is extinguished and replaced with another contract and a third party. However, you can also use this for subject-to, seller finance, hybrid wraps, agreement for sale, and lease options.

A novation agreement is not technically subject-to, because you don't close escrow, but all the other options do close escrow. In real estate, a novation happens when a third party enters into an agreement to replace a departing part of the contract. The idea here is that you don't want to own the property for a long time, but there is room within the equity to sell it on the retail market. In addition to subject-to and other long-term deals, I occasionally do fix-and-flips this way because I can bring in an additional $40,000 or so per month. I can use this amount for entry fee payments or other things. This is particularly useful when a homeowner wants a bigger piece of the pie and they're willing to wait for payment. I generally give them a set amount, then I take whatever extra I can make when I sell the house retail.

Here's a typical flip example on a wholesale deal: Let's say a wholesaler comes to me with a property that costs $150,000 with an ARV of $225,000 and repair costs around $25,000. If I list the property for $225,000 and subtract about 7 percent (1 percent to my wife, who is my agent, 3 percent to the buyer's agent, and 3 percent closing costs), there's about $209,250 to play with after the sale. Of that, however, there are the purchasing costs: $3,000 in closing costs, lender fees (which could include 12 percent interest, which is about $7,000 on top of the original $150,000), and I still need a down payment—a lender is not going to give me 100 percent of what I need. I need $25,000 in cash just to buy the property and this doesn't even include remodel fees.

See how complicated this is just for the acquisition? See how many numbers you need to account for to make the deal work? I haven't even started the renovation yet, so all of that has to work out perfectly just to avoid additional costs.

Let's take a step back. This means you have to come in with $50,000 up front just to break into the industry. You can't do this on a credit card, so you have to have your own money or you need a gap lender or some other sort of connection just to get a loan. But is it worth it? Oftentimes, yes.

However, what if you could do this without having all of these complications? What I recommend is doing a subject-to-retail deal. Let's remove some of these complications. I plan to acquire the house and list it for $225,000, but subtract the remodel fee, the closing costs, and the Realtor fees, and I get $209,250. Rather than getting a loan just to get another loan, I talk to the seller about doing a temporary seller finance deal. If I can buy the property subject-to, the debt is already in place and there's way more money to keep in my pocket. The acquisition is coming from owner financing or subject-to. The debt is there so there's no need to get a higher-interest loan to pay off a lower-interest loan. Then I can avoid all these lender fees and just raise private money for the renovation, which is $25,000. On the front end, it's less exposure and less risk and more money. Currently, I'm only doing fix-and-flips if the seller allows for us to keep the debt in place for the remainder of the flip. It's much less complicated, and once the seller is educated on how it works, they're likely to be on board.

What's the difference between a sub-tail and a novation agreement? On a sub-tail, you close escrow and take ownership of the property. The seller gets their money up front and they're no longer attached to the deal. On a novation agreement, everybody gets paid at the end. The real difference is whether you want to be the owner of the property. You can also bring in higher margins if you don't have to close escrow in the first place. Primarily, we buy novation agreements and subject-to, then take those retail.

Traditional Rental Exit Strategies

Everyone pretty much understands the concept of a rental. It's a basic idea. You buy a property and then rent it out at a higher rate per month. For rentals, you can use:

- Subject-to.
- Seller finance.
- Hybrid wraps.
- Lease options.
- Agreement for sale.

It's a widely used exit strategy, but there are pros and cons. You're going to need to own the property and many people think you must have a lot of cash up front. Most people like to use the BRRRR (buy, rehab, rent, refinance, repeat) method; personally, I like to use the SRRR (sub-to, rehab, rent, repeat) method, but this also requires some capital. That said, it has fewer moving parts and it's one of the simplest exit strategies.

In this scenario, the seller sells to me a property subject-to. Let's say the price is $150,000 and the entry fee is about $15,000. I either have to have my own money or I need to raise the money to get in. With a renter, there's no up-front fee. The renter typically only pays the first month and the security deposit. With this exit strategy, you also must consider vacant months and any additional marketing you have to do to get a renter.

For a lot of new people, rentals are not the best strategy to begin with. But, when you are thinking long-term, you should have some rentals in your portfolio so you can make consistent money over time. You also need to put some money aside for any problems the renters might have. Renters are notoriously rough on rental properties. They break things and things break on their own. You're going to have to worry about these properties all the time. Renters trash houses and there's the possibility of frequent turnover, evictions, and other headaches. But, of course, there are benefits. You get tax benefits. You get cash flow. And no one can buy the property from you, which is the opposite of a lease option, where you might lose this cash flow stream after the five-year agreement ends and the buyer is still interested in the deal.

Group Home Exit Strategies

Next, there's the group home exit strategy. I own a few assisted living and behavioral health homes. "Group home" is sort of a general term for all of these, but I don't like to get involved with models that have government oversight or that require a full-time staff of nurses, so I try to focus on group homes or temporary housing when I do these types of deals. For group homes, you can do agreement for sale, hybrid wraps, lease options, seller finance, and subject-to. Primarily, these tenants are going to be people in need. This can be a silver lining for all parties involved. There could be mental needs. There could be physical needs. I get referrals from companies like CBI (Community Bridges, Inc.) or PIR (Partners in Recovery), two Arizona companies that help people with needs connect to homes like these. When I buy a property subject-to, I can reach out to companies like these to help me fill these homes with those in need.

Here's what's unique about the group home model: Let's say we've got a three-bedroom/two-bath home in Phoenix. The typical rent for a house that size is $1,500 per month, but when you have a group home, you can take this same exact house and make it worth $3,500 per month. In a three-bed/two-bath home, we can get nine people at $650 per bed. You can have multiple beds per room in this house.

This money comes from Social Security Income or Social Security Disability Income, Medicaid Special Assistance, or Private Pay. And you don't need to have a specialized license like you would with assisted living or behavioral health facilities. You also do not have to have chefs or nurses or anything like that. You just need to have a business license and talk over your plans with your insurance company so everything is on the up-and-up. For more specifics, reach out to companies like CBI and PIR in your area and they'll not only tell you where to start and how to run this business, but they'll also recommend other group home business owners whom you might be able to wholesale to if you decide not to manage the home yourself.

Vacation Rental Exit Strategies

Whether you use Airbnb or Vrbo, there are countless things to think about with a vacation rental. Personally, I avoided this path for a long time because it's easy to oversaturate a market and there's always the possibility of something like the COVID-19 pandemic happening and leaving you with a pile of mortgages and little income.

That said, I have expanded my Airbnb territory and I work with Noah Hoffman on these deals, because I don't like to deal with customers. Noah, an Airbnb expert you may have seen from my social media posts, handles everything and I pay him per home per month to do so.

Let's talk about this exit strategy. You can acquire a house with subject-to, seller finance, wraps, lease options, and agreements for sale. Then you can go out and turn it into a vacation rental. I'll go over the specifics of this in Chapter 8, but I'll cover some of the basics here.

The first rule of doing an Airbnb is to base everything on the rental rate. If you can't cash flow at the rental rate, in my opinion, you shouldn't take on the property. The second rule is that you need to have capital. You have to market and furnish and maintain the property. Third, you should get a partner. Work with someone who knows what they're doing because the Airbnb model can be a lot of work, but if you can get someone to manage the property and share the profits with, then that's a good situation. Then you don't have to work on assigning cleaners, responding when the Wi-Fi goes out, and all those other little pesky tasks.

INVESTOR STORY

Sam Singh—Former Wholesaler
"What's your long-term goal?"

Sam Singh lives in Fresno, California. He's relatively new to the creative side of the business but he's about to close his fortieth deal. It wasn't until this deal that he brought into the community as a wholesaler where he was pushed to start looking into creative deals. "What's your long-term goal? What's next season look like?" he was asked by a fellow student. With creative deals, and with a longer vision on expanding his tool kit, he can build true, long-term wealth. Part of this comes from personal branding. Sam would tell you, "You don't raise private capital, you attract it."

This deal is a hybrid deal in Henderson, Nevada, right outside of Vegas. The owner, an older seller in his eighties, had a problem tenant who hadn't paid in two years. The tenant was his stepson, who was married and had three daughters, and who wanted to take advantage of his parents. The lease agreement had expired, so the seller was paying losing money on the mortgage and utilities and paying from his retirement savings. The stepson was also emotionally manipulating his father and mother, letting them go into foreclosure rather than pay the rent he owed.

The lead came from a cold call to the pre-foreclosure list. Sam had been in escrow for the deal for the past six months. Out of respect to the stepfather and mother, who had begged Sam not to throw the family out, he had given them the benefit of the doubt. He asked fourteen Realtors to help the stepson and his family find a new place and put some money in their pocket, but the stepson continued to use the three daughters as emotional hostages: "If you toss us out, you're tossing them on the street."

The purchase price was $305,000 for the house, which was likely worth $415,000 or so. It was half sub-to and half seller equity. The Henderson market had been hit somewhat hard, so the valuation had dropped recently. Regardless, in this scenario, creative finance was the only option. The tenant had threatened everybody, including Realtors, escrow officers, and everyone else who came across his path. Sam leaned on some colleagues in the Nevada area and found out that the deal was good, but it's possible to hemorrhage money during closing. He knew the guy was going to trash the place, and even if he sued the seller, it wouldn't matter, he was going to lose.

The seller would break into tears nearly every time he spoke with Sam. He couldn't believe what his stepson had turned into. And, if that weren't enough, his wife had recently gotten Alzheimer's and no longer recognized him. With all of this going on, the tenant continued to not care and allowed his parents to go into foreclosure. The father's response? "We'll sell it, but we want half the money." For Sam, most of his deals are easy, but this had been eating away at everyone involved for six months or longer.

Sam planned to give the investor who brought him the deal a larger portion than normal. He was giving her $10,000 in the entry fee and some of the cash flow from the property. Sam got on the phone with the stepson. Sam told him that he would give him a few thousand dollars and he could move on, or else his own stepfather would evict him and that would be it. Or Sam could evict on him or file on him for trespassing. After that call, the stepson called his stepfather saying Sam was harassing him. More manipulation. As a long-term deal, the property would cash flow for $400 or make a little more as an Airbnb, but Sam could also sell it to a hedge fund and make $100,000. But, focusing on the long-term goal, Sam told the seller he could take on the eviction himself and stick to cash flow.

In the end, the seller told him he would take $40,000 less just to make sure Sam went through with the eviction and he could walk away completely from the house and the stepson.

This is still in process, but Sam plans to hold the deal and re-fuses to let the stepson win so the seller can walk away from the investment.

KEY TAKEAWAY | Don't let lesser goals push you in the wrong direction. Double down on your long-term goals and alter the path along the way to make it happen.

CHAPTER 7

Where to Find Deals

"I'm on the pursuit of happiness and I know /
Everything that shine ain't always gonna be gold."

—KID CUDI, "PURSUIT OF HAPPINESS"

Deals can come from everywhere. I get deals from real estate agents.
I get deals from expired listings. I get deals from tired landlords. I
get deals from probate attorneys. I get deals from social media. And
nearly half of my deals come from pre-foreclosures, because people
have a tremendous amount of pain and they need help. It falls down
to the Four Pillars of a Good Lead.

1. Timing
2. Price/Terms
3. Motivation to Sell
4. Condition

But, for now, what you need to decide is what type of investor
you want to be and how that fits into the neighborhoods where you
want to do deals. Research your area and the other areas you want
to do deals in and see what kinds of deals are being done. Research
your zip codes. Talk to other people who have rental properties in
your area. Squad up with people in our online community and also

in your local community. Use online tools to see how you can find buyers in the area and do your research to see how deals are being done around you.

No matter what type of business you build, leads only come from five paths.

1. Direct to seller
2. Direct to market/agent
3. Direct to referral partner
4. Wholesalers with dead leads
5. Work for someone else

That's it. Everything you've ever heard of—postcards, Realtors, driving for dollars, cold-calling—falls into one of these five categories.

Not long ago, a real estate agent contacted me with a potential deal. The agent said they had two clients in Jackson, Mississippi, who said, "I just want to dump these properties." She couldn't sell the listings and called me to see if I could take them off her hands with a creative finance deal. I asked if they were hemorrhaging money or cash-flowing or what the issue was. The agent said the sellers owned them free and clear and each was worth about $100,000, but the owners weren't making money because they were investing it back into other properties. In reality, this wasn't true (the sellers were either lying to the Realtor or lying to themselves). The reality was that they were in a high-crime area.

Generally speaking, renters in high-crime areas damage properties. This means you're always going to have repairs and you're always going to have vacancies. This sounded like a great deal from the initial pitch, but it just wasn't worth the hassle for me at the time. But you have to do the research to figure out whether or not something is too good to be true. I decided I didn't want to jump through all of the hoops to make this deal work.

Do your research on the areas you want to buy in so you know when and where to find good deals. Sometimes the answer is obvious. Sometimes less so. Jamil Damji, my costar on *Triple Digit Flip*, likes to buy properties within certain zip codes, but also only on certain roads within those zip codes, so his buy box is focused and specific. The more you know, the more niche your portfolio can be. This is somewhat of a luxury, because we live in the Phoenix area, which is a hot spot for real estate. But you need to go where the deals are if you're going to make it in this business. You don't want to open a Ferrari dealership in a tiny town where people can't afford Ferraris. You need to do deals where people are making deals.

There's an old joke about a man losing his keys at night in a parking lot. He lost his keys near where his car was parked, but he's looking for his keys across the parking lot in the area with better lighting. When someone asks him what he's doing, he says, "I lost my keys over there but the lighting is better over here." You have to let go of your preconceived notions and go where the deals are. Otherwise, you're wasting your time and stalling your better future.

My major goal as an investor is to buy 1,000 houses in good areas with creative finance. But this doesn't mean I don't regularly pass on deals that don't fit my criteria. There were two times when I didn't listen to my gut and did deals based on cash flow alone. Right away, I regretted doing those deals. You have to think about management. You have to think about the headache. You have to double-check and triple-check the cash flow. Will it cash flow? Is it going to appreciate? What's your exit strategy? These things matter. It's not about closing deals to close deals. It's about creating a plan for your portfolio and consistently refining that vision to build wealth and better your business.

I get this question a lot: What would you do if you were stripped of all your assets and only had a $100 bill to start over? This is a fun scenario for entrepreneurs. But what I would do is spend that money on a dozen doughnuts, then go to a Goodwill store and buy a bike. Then I would bike over to a title company or closing attorney and ask for a free list of pre-foreclosure homes. These lists aren't super accurate in terms of the most recent data—they're often a week or two old, so sometimes include properties that have already sold—but they are free, so they're a good place to start. I'd put the list in a mapping program on a computer at the library and print it out (you can also do this on your smartphone). I'd use the last bit of money for a burner phone and then get to work knocking on doors, collecting leads, and making calls.

I would knock on at least twenty doors a day. After about a hundred doors, I would get a contract. Those are the basic odds. I still have my tool kit, so once I found out the seller's situation, I could do wholesale, creative finance, subject-to, or lease option, but the point is, it's really simple to get a free list and start door knocking. But simple doesn't mean easy. This is where mindset comes in. Even veterans in the business can be hesitant to knock doors. The best door knockers are so good because they're consistent and they're fearless.

Now let's talk more about key performance indicators. I've touched on it briefly, but what do we really look for? In the example above, let's say I did get one deal for every hundred houses. That's a pretty simple model that should scale. I would get about 1 percent across the board. To dig deeper, there would be better neighborhoods and worse neighborhoods, but that's why we're tracking our actions with data. As business guru Peter Drucker said, "What gets measured gets managed."

In Arizona, when a brand-new person joins my team, I expect that if they go out and knock on 150 doors, then they'll get around three or four appointments. We have this data because we've repeated it thousands of times. A dozen or so people will meet up at our offices on a Saturday morning (volunteers and paid staff), go over some basic door-knocking strategies, and then start canvassing neighborhoods to find deals. Again, it's simple but not necessarily easy. The difficulty, of course, is consistency. Like a batting average or three-pointer percentage, there's a lot of rejection on your journey to success.

I have four people on staff who regularly knock doors. Their only goal is to set up an appointment. They set appointments for a closer, who then closes deals. Again, this is a scaled operation, so don't get overwhelmed with these numbers. Start by either knocking on doors yourself or hiring one person to do it for you. It's something that you will get better at over time. If we step back for a moment, a new door knocker gets one appointment for every fifty doors knocked, on average. If they knock on 150 doors in a day, they should get three appointments. These are numbers for inexperienced knockers.

Experienced knockers can get four appointments for every hundred doors they knock, so that's one appointment for every twenty-five doors. Why? What's the difference? Experienced people move a little faster, know what to look for, and have a better understanding of what's not being said. Like cold callers or anything else where you can gather some experience, judgment calls happen faster and it's easier to tell whether or not a person's situation equals a deal. The same is true for closing rates. If you put in the work, you will inevitably get better over time.

Now let's talk about hangers and notes, because not everyone is going to be home. That's expected, so what do you do then? We leave a point of contact on every single door. A lot of deals come from these notes. Some teams use nice printed documents or laminated hangers, but we like to leave more of a personal touch. We either do a handwritten note or even just a scrap of paper. It might say, "We were doing a renovation in your area and wanted to see if your house might be for sale." (For us, this is often the case, so revise based on your experience and reality.) Leave your name and number. Like a bandit sign, you want to look less experienced. People in foreclosure do not want to deal with another big company, so don't look like one. I also don't like to spend money on leave-behinds. Our key performance indicators (KPIs) indicate that of every hundred leave-behinds, one person will call if we leave a hanger, but two people will call after a handwritten sticky note. This increases your chance of a call because these people don't want to deal with a bank or some other public entity. They'd rather deal with a neighbor. That's the point. We either use a sticky note or a three-by-five index card with Scotch tape. We tape the card to the door or we leave it in the driver's side door or window of their car. We do this because people are more likely to look at a note on their car door than their front door; some people don't even use the main door of their house. But the main thing is making a point of contact. This is how you build a business. This is how you scale.

I know 1–2 percent may not sound like a lot, but we get a ton of deals this way and any individual deal can be worth tens of thousands of dollars. It's a numbers game. I once talked to a woman who had learned how to do door knocking online, but she wasn't closing deals. She saw me and my team talking about door knocking on Facebook and saw that we were getting deals done. She wanted to know what she was doing wrong. I let her shadow my team and we figured out there were a few things she was doing wrong. She was leaving professional business cards on the front doors of houses. Before the end of the day, she got a call from one of the earlier drops using handwritten notes and it was the first deal she ever got. She watched us leave the note, contact the seller, and close the deal. A lot of deals come from this method, so we make it part of our conveyor belt system. I want ongoing leads, so I structure a system for that to happen. Without leads, you don't have a business.

What Makes a House Distressed?

"How do I get started in real estate?" This is the most common question I get. Like any entrepreneurial venture, there are countless ways to get started, but in order to simplify things, I want to focus on the two most common ways: driving for dollars, aka driving for deals (manual but close to free), and cold-calling leads (automatic but somewhat costly).

Driving for dollars is the cheapest possible way to get started in real estate. If you have no money and lots of time, this is the method for you. Let's get started: What does it mean to drive for dollars? Essentially, driving for dollars is a method in real estate investing where you look for distressed properties or motivated sellers to work with. We're looking for off-market deals to either wholesale or fix-and-flip, but what we're really looking for are motivated sellers.

Logistically, the way this works is that you want to either walk or drive through neighborhoods and then write down or record addresses that appear to be distressed. You can use a pen and paper. You can use an app. You can use an online document. Minimum, you need to write down the address, but it's also a good idea to write any notes, take a photo, and record the date you found the property. This is your initial groundwork to get started; feel free to make adjustments as you find what works for you.

What are you looking for when you make notes to find deals? There are countless telltale signs that a property is distressed. Some of the basics include overgrown lawns, boarded-up windows, holes in the roof or other deteriorating elements of the exterior, mail or advertisements piled up, or bank notices on the front door. Once you track this information, you can start to gather a little research on the property. This would include the property address and also the owner's mailing address. It's possible the owner is a tired landlord, a bank, or someone who inherited the property, and this house is now a hassle for them.

Look, we've all seen distressed homes at one point or another. Most of us just think, "Wow, this is a bad area," and we keep driving to wherever we're going. If you're going to make it in this business, you need to act on these opportunities. Not long ago, we organized a challenge called Driving for Deals (also known as the Get Your First Deal Challenge) in my online community. We helped about fifty people get their first deal in the first week and another 300 close on deals over the course of the challenge.

Let's talk more about what to look for and where to look for it. Not every distressed home is going to be worth a ton of money. If you drive by a row of vacant, crappy houses, you need to ask yourself why they're that way. This could be a high-crime area. It could have something to do with construction in the area. But it doesn't matter where you are. What matters is that you can find "ugly" houses anywhere and everywhere. If you're going on a journey to find distressed properties, you should be able to find fifty to one hundred distressed homes on your first day, as long as you give yourself a couple of hours and use the strategies in this book and possibly an app to track these homes.

From what I've seen over the years, about 70 percent of brand-new wholesalers drive for dollars. That's how they get their first deal.

They're looking for a distressed home and finding people who have pain points or signals of distress or a situation in which they're going to give you a good deal on a property. When I started in real estate, I had to learn these signs on my own. The distressed-home part is the easy part. The hard part is talking to sellers, negotiating a deal, and working to either close on the deal yourself or set that seller up with a buyer and make money on the transaction as a wholesaler. This is the reason we did the challenge, because we were able to set up newbies with information and collaborators. With the right software, the right technique, and the right connections, driving for dollars can be easy.

Let's talk about recent activity. It's one thing to find an ugly house in the middle of nowhere where no one is going to want to buy it or live in it. It's something else entirely to find an ugly house in an area of recent activity. I'm talking about areas where investors are already doing deals. When you're in your car or virtually driving for dollars online, you will start to find nice, newly updated houses—known as a path of progress—where investors and homeowners are coming in and turning the old into new. They're buying older homes, painting them, working on the curb appeal, and expanding the neighborhood. All of a sudden, a home from the 1920s looks brand-new. Investor activity like this means the path of progress is expanding and there's room for you or your collaborators to expand the market. This is also true for new builds, apartment complexes, and other developments.

You drive around and look for opportunities. It's that simple. You find these opportunities next to or adjacent to the path of progress. If you need more of a visual, in my webinar "Find Your First 500 Deals for Free," I broke down some of my habits and we went out in the field to discuss potential deals. At the first house, I noticed the landscaping had been neglected and the grass was overgrown, but I want to find multiple signs of distress in order to consider it a distressed home.

I usually look for two to five signs of distress; these might be hoarder situations, junk in the yard, broken-down cars, busted windows, and so on. In the webinar, I found a series of owners along the route who were clearly going through something. At one house, I noticed a broken-down F-150 with a busted window next to piles of trash and some damaged yard equipment. These are all clear signs of distress. Two houses up, there was a house with boarded-up windows, broken glass, overgrown weeds, and various other signs of distress.

We also found two houses next to each other that I now have under contract. There were buckets of oil next to the trash from the previous owner. The windows were boarded up. There were doors sitting outside, unattached to the house. There were pieces of Astroturf rather than a lawn. There was a Christmas tree in the yard in March. There was a shopping cart and even signs that a squatter was living in the house. I decided to make an offer on the deal, removed the signs of distress, and was able to make about $20,000 assigning the house to a fix-and-flipper who will make money once he fixes it up and sells it.

Next door, we were able to turn another abandoned house into a duplex. But what's really cool is that there is enough land to build a second duplex on the same lot, so we can double our eventual passive income with this deal. If that's not cool enough, I paid Katie, the woman who found these three properties in a Driving for Deals challenge, about $30,000 for bringing these deals to me. All of these homes were in the path of progress so we know there are going to be comps and opportunities to make these deals work.

Those are the basics, but what is the best method by which to drive for dollars? You're going to hear me say this over and over, but it's all about creating a system you can plug into and be consistent. You have to take immediate action. You have to do it day after day. The best way to get started is to identify your target areas, create a system to canvas the neighborhood, and collect this initial data. Being organized from the beginning will make you more efficient over time, but you have to get started in order to grow, so don't overcomplicate the process. Just get out there and get to work. Using this method will help you find deals and become profitable quickly, but having a marketing system and strong negotiation skills are what will lead to results. This means tracking your efforts. This means improving your negotiation skills.

Door Knocking = Deal Flow

A tremendous amount of my deal flow comes from door knocking. When I first started, I did this on my own. As the business scaled, I grew a door knocking team and utilized a door knocking app in order to create consistency and congruency among the team members. Let's break down why door knocking is so profitable, especially for those on a limited budget or early in their real estate investment careers.

I know a guy in Fresno, California, who does nothing but door knocking. He took home a million dollars in 2018 and another million in 2019 just knocking on doors. This strategy works. There is so much money to be made in door knocking that it's insane.

To begin, let's talk about KPIs, or key performance indicators. A performance indicator is a type of measurement to help evaluate the success or failure of a particular activity. In real estate, everything can be tracked with a KPI and nearly everything can deliver a win if you understand your numbers and put in the work.

Door knocking is coming back in a big way. With phone carriers and text messages being more and more regulated, door knocking is a tried-and-true approach where the only real limit is you. When we talk about text blasts and cold calls, there are lawsuits happening all over the country. They see this as solicitation. This doesn't mean you can't do it—I'll go over both as successful methods—but it does mean you have to be careful. But door knocking has zero regulation. Nobody can tell you that you can't knock on their door. We even knock on doors that say "No solicitation," because solicitation is about selling them something; we're not convincing them to buy, we're convincing them to sell. When you explain this, you turn the conversation in an instant.

We use the best data and the best systems that exist for cold-calling and text blasting, but the overall response has still been cut in half over the past couple of years. This is because the carriers—Verizon, T-Mobile, Sprint, etc.—are tracking the type of language used in these text blasts and marking them as spam. Google does the same thing with email. But again, no one is out there blocking you from knocking on a door. It's analog, not digital.

Successful investors will be door knocking for multiple reasons going forward. It's the fastest way to get a contract. With cold-calling, the average campaign takes two months to get a deal. That includes hiring a cold caller, building a list, filling the pipeline, and following up. With door knocking, I've gotten contracts within forty-five minutes. Not only are you there in person but you also remove the disconnect of the telephone. Potential sellers see that you are a real person and there to help. You can shake their hand. You can have a real conversation. You can gain their trust. All of these aspects mean you can get a deal quickly.

Besides gassing up your car and buying an app to help you manage your door knocking, there's no real marketing budget needed for door knocking. This way, even in a bad economy where texts and cold calls and direct mail can be expensive, door knocking will always be there. In addition to less overhead, we've discovered you also get better deals.

From my team's KPIs, we've discovered that our average wholesale deal with cold-calling is $13,000–$15,000, but when we do door knocking, the average net profit is around $25,000, nearly double the amount of cold-calling. Why? Because there's a higher level of trust, we're there in person, and people can't just hang up on us, so we have more room to negotiate. Because they have to go through the awkwardness of simply standing in front of another person, we get to do our pitch and have the chance to close a better deal.

This also helps with creative finance deals. One of the things I do best is explain creative finance to sellers, but it's much harder over the phone than it is in person. You can do it over email or over FaceTime even, but being in someone's living room with a legal pad is much more efficient. People like visuals. In fact, if someone feels hesitant, one thing I do is have them restructure the terms just to make sure they understand my explanation and we're on the same page. In person, this is dramatically easier than it is over the phone.

Expired Listings on the Multiple Listing Service (MLS)

If you don't want to spend a ton of money on county record lists and don't have time to drive around, looking for expired listings is a way to find homes for sale. These homeowners are in pain because they've essentially already been told their house is not wanted on the market. The home is either not worth what they want or they had an equity situation where they couldn't get what they needed to get out of the deal. This happens more frequently in economic downtimes. It is a bad situation for the seller, but a good situation for you, because you don't have to be the one to tell them they're not going to get the price they want in a traditional manner since the market has already told them.

What is an expired listing? It's a property that hasn't been sold by the end of a period stipulated in the listing agreement between the seller and listing agent. The seller decides they want to sell for whatever reason, so they go out and find a real estate agent. Generally speaking, the seller gives the agent about six months to sell a property and they sign a contract that has all of this in writing. Sometimes there's a buyout clause that lets the seller exit the contract early for a small fee, but this is more on a situational, case-by-case basis. Either way, expired listings can work for you.

After six months or so if the agent was unable to sell for the price, the agent loses their agreement with the seller and they no longer have control over the property; they have no right to sell the property. Sometimes the agent will ask to extend the listing for another six months, but this is somewhat rare and perhaps based on the housing market at the time. Once the listing truly expires, the seller can now sell the house without having to pay the agent a fee. This can happen the day after the listing expires.

In one scenario, a homeowner was getting offers of $70,000 from cash buyers, but they wanted more money. They had an agent list the property for $110,000 on the MLS. They didn't get an offer, but when this deal came to me, I was able to offer $120,000 in a creative finance deal. Why would anyone do this? They wanted to make a certain number and I knew I could make that number work on a month-to-month basis, plus I offered $10,000 extra because I wanted a zero percent interest rate on the creative finance loan. This works best when the seller has a tremendous amount of equity, but there are many ways to make creative finance deals work.

The pro of an expired listing is that you can step in and solve a ton of problems for the seller. They've been through the headache of listing their home on an open market for six months and either no one made an offer or no one made an offer they liked, so you can do a creative deal that works for everyone. If a seller used the MLS and an agent, which means tens of thousands of people likely saw the house and they still couldn't sell it, they're going to be more apt to negotiate, and they're doing it from a weaker position. An expired listing does all of this pre-negotiating for you, plus you can be a superhero for this person by taking this headache off their hands.

That said, there are still cons and obstacles, as with any type of deal. The seller could simply have a number that is too aggressive in mind. Maybe the home has sentimental value for them. Maybe they're just in debt in a bad market. Whatever the case, the seller could be difficult and not willing to negotiate. This doesn't mean you can't make a deal, but this is a situation where your negotiating and your bag of creative finance tricks need to be on point. You might find yourself making a deal over asking price on a house that needs a ton of work. I've done this many times because I knew I could get zero percent down, and then I have an opportunity to find any number of exit strategies to make the deal work.

One house I bought in this situation turned out to have an illegal addition on the back. This meant homeowners didn't want to touch it and certain banks wouldn't lend loans until this was addressed. But, for us, we were adding this deal to our rental portfolio, so this problem didn't matter (see a similar story in Chapter 5). I care about being able to pay the mortgage with renters. I care about earning cash flow.

Now that you better understand this strategy, let's talk about getting a list of expired listings. In our market, we work with what I like to call Unicorn Realtors. These agents work with investors and understand investing and creative finance. They're able to pull these lists for us from the MLS. One easy way to find Unicorn Realtors is through the BiggerPockets agent directory—you can be connected (for free!) with investor-friendly agents in your market of choice at www.biggerpockets.com/agent/match. You can also talk to escrow officers within your title company. What you want to ask for is expired listings within the last sixty to ninety days, and then you can skip-trace this list, which will get all of the owners' phone numbers. If you don't have money for marketing, you can also take this list and knock on doors. Like we said before, when you show your face and go directly to the seller, you have a better opportunity to make these deals work. Like any good deal, we want good terms, cash flow, and good location.

For the real estate agent, you're creating a relationship and showing that you're a problem solver. If you present yourself in the right way, you can be an ongoing solution for real estate agents who know that certain sellers have a pipe dream offer they're never going to get on the market. You can pay smaller referral fees, perhaps $500 rather than thousands in commissions, and it's a win-win scenario. For the seller, you simply need to solve their problem.

Cold-Calling and Texting

One of the most effective ways to create a consistent chain of leads comes from cold-calling and texting. These are two different strategies, but they're similar. If we start with a text, we immediately want to get the seller on the phone. Getting on the phone is a big part of your success. I want to discuss using a dialer, the benefits of cold-calling, KPIs to track numbers, and even how to use a virtual assistant (VA) to create a conveyer belt of hot leads when you're ready to scale.

A dialer or autodialer is a software that automatically dials telephone numbers. Then, when a seller answers, the dialer stops dialing to either play a recorded message or connect the recipient to a live rep from your company. My team generally uses a three-number dialer and, this way, a VA can make hundreds of calls in a day, speak with a dozen or so sellers, and potentially book up to eight leads based on the area and the list they're calling from. You can use your own phone number if you have a small list, but if you use your own number on a large list and manually dial, you're going to get frustrated and you're likely going to get your number marked as spam. It's also nearly impossible to remember details for everyone's phone number in your cell phone, so you'll be getting calls back and not know who you are speaking with or forget which house they're calling about. We use three numbers at a time and rotate those out as we need to based on feedback from the programs we use and updated carrier restrictions.

With an autodialer, you can be more efficient; you can call multiple lines at once, and it's impossible to call the same number of people manually in the same time period. Plus you can use numbers with the area codes of the areas you're calling. This is pretty standard today, but people want to see local numbers. When I first started, I used a multi-dialer to triple my calls. It was much faster. It went from having five or six calls in a day to thirty to forty in a day. My VAs might make a hundred calls or more in a day. The dialer also tells you who is calling back, plus you can input notes about the conversation. You're going to be asking specific questions, so you need to be able to take notes and gather information. For the most part, you won't get a sale on the first call. On average, it takes seven calls to the seller, because you're building rapport and creating a relationship. This doesn't mean it's impossible to close on the first call, but it is more likely to take multiple calls. That's why you need to be consistent. This is also why we use VAs to help us do all of these rudimentary steps to bring in leads.

Let's take a step back and talk about my team's overall strategy. We select a target niche and then gather a list of contacts from that niche. We then skip-trace the niche list to gather leads. Depending on which program you have, you may also need to scrub the list after you skip-trace to look for multiples. Then we import the list to a dialer and use the dialer to start making calls. As conversions start to come in, we work those deals until we can start to lock them up.

As for the niche, we may stack up a list of vacants with a list of pre-foreclosures. In the program we use, we can choose our area with a zip code or even trace a location on a map. Then we can start to filter by things like occupancy status, mailing status, classification, property type, on market or off market, ownership info, and estimated value. One way to get started might be searching for criteria like mailing vacant (this means the owner receives mail at a location other than the address of the home), owned for ten years, and a value less than $350,000. All of this depends on your area and niche, so you want to play with these numbers and values to figure out who might be willing to sell. We're going to talk more about situational lists in Chapter 8, but there's no magic formula. You have to try a few things to get a good list for where you want to do business. It's a numbers game.

This probably sounds a little overwhelming, so let's talk about some real-world examples. During my Zero to Hero Challenge, we created a fifteen-day live event so hundreds of people could watch my team use these methods to lock up deals. We picked an area where we hadn't done business before—Charlotte, North Carolina—and started a new real estate investment business from scratch. Over the course of the event, we created an LLC, launched a website, built out a niche list, and booked two virtual assistants from StartVirtual to make calls for us. During this time frame, we closed on three properties and brought in $70,000 in cash.

This method costs more money than driving for dollars, but it's super effective. You must decide if you have more time or more money when you're just starting out. For my business, we love to have multiple streams of leads, so it makes sense for us to do all of the methods mentioned in this book. That's how we grew to over 300 doors and countless flips and wholesale deals in just a few years.

Looking at these numbers, I can gather four to six leads in an eight-hour day and convert about one in thirty leads, but a virtual assistant can get one to three leads in an eight-hour day and convert one in forty-five of these leads. For the leads to convert, meaning it turns into a deal, the timing has to be right, the sale amount has to be right, motivation has to be there, and the house has to fit my criteria. This is how we bring in regular leads. The industry standard is about one in fifty conversions, but we've raised our close rates to about one in thirty on average.

For our VAs, we want them to bring in, on average, two leads per day; this means they may bring in one lead on Monday and three on Tuesday. If no one from our acquisition team steps in, they can only close about one of these leads completely per day on average. When I say close, I mean put the house under contract. This means we lose 50 percent of our conversions, but we also gain back a great deal of time. I don't have time to make calls eight hours a day, and I don't want to make cold calls all day, so we balance out these KPIs with our goals to close the number of deals we need to close on a consistent basis. There's also a huge difference in talking to qualified leads a VA brings us versus talking to people who do not want to sell. It's just not a good use of your time, so hire someone else to do it when you can afford to do so. Bring in some leverage so you can focus on the aspects of the business you do best.

StartVirtual, a company I partner with and now co-own, uses virtual assistants in the Philippines willing to call in your time frame. StartVirtual trains them and manages them. They let you lead them, but they also have training systems in place and a customer success manager to help lead when you're unavailable. Plus, it only costs you $7–$12 an hour to bring in these leads rather than wasting your valuable time. We continue to evolve this system over time and currently have cold callers who bring in about thirty to sixty hot leads a day.

Cold-calling is a great lead source when you're consistent. But it does cost money and it does take time to set up. Another option is texting. Again, you can do this yourself or you can bring in a virtual assistant, but the key is to be consistent. I'm not going to go too far into the weeds here with texting because regulations are constantly changing and I encourage you to look for my most recent videos about texting on YouTube. I will go over some of the principles here and encourage you to consistently focus on getting better as your business grows.

My business uses specific platforms—currently BatchLeads and BatchDialer—because they stay up to date with carrier restrictions and have been the most effective compared to other platforms. With these programs, we can get into the conversation faster. In just a few minutes, you can set up a system and start talking to sellers. One major benefit is that you can tap into sellers who don't pick up random numbers, which is becoming commonplace with people today. You can also get super-raw information from sellers right away. We buy four to six deals per month from texting sellers and we average another four to six deals from creative finance. Personally, I don't answer cold calls, but I never miss a text message. That said, we use both to bring in leads.

Texting costs money and, depending on the platform you use, you need to make sure you are compliant with carriers. Some programs let you send out 5,000 texts in a blast, but this is not compliant with industry standards. With the program we use, someone does have to manually click the button on a computer for each text, but it's a safer way to not get blocked and to bring in leads. Again, we have virtual assistants do this, so it's their time, not our time. But you want to be compliant, because you are dealing with people. You want to reach out as a person, not just a spammy business. Doing less in the beginning also helps you gather data in an effective way, meaning you can alter your messages and make changes to increase conversions as your data starts to come in.

If I'm messaging numbers on a list, I may just say something like, "Hey [name], my name is Pace. Is [address] still for sale?" The programs we use allow us to compose about ten standard messages and cycle through those messages. They're really basic. Don't send a paragraph. Don't say too much. Think about it like dating. Say just enough to get the conversation going, then focus on your follow-up. Based on our data, we've found that the best time for texting on weekdays is from 4:00 p.m. to 7:00 p.m., when people are generally done with their nine-to-five jobs and are more likely to answer. For Saturdays, the best time is generally after 10:00 a.m. We will text up until 8:30 p.m. In our business, we don't bother sellers on Sundays.

That's what works for us. I don't want to bother people and I don't want to be bothered on Sunday, but that's a choice for you to make. Keep your messages short. Reply quickly to get the ball rolling. Move to a call when you can. And keep following up until they give you a price. Our basic path is to create an introduction and confirm the address, then we ask if they would consider an offer, then we ask to hop on a call. If they express interest, get them on the phone.

If you're doing this yourself, you need to make time to respond to these messages. Some individuals only send out five to ten texts an hour so they have time to respond. You don't want to wait thirty minutes or more to respond. It's ideal to respond within five minutes. That said, you might get a response days or weeks later, so you also shouldn't throw away leads even if they're not interested right away. With our cold-calling and texting campaigns, we've recycled lists months later and brought in high-caliber leads because those people who weren't interested are ready to sell. It's about their current situation, and current situations are always changing. Stick with it. Be the one there when they're ready to sell.

Think of yourself as a corporation. Why do you see McDonald's and Coca-Cola on television all of the time? Everyone knows these companies exist, but they want to be in front of you with billboards, radio ads, and television ads so when you're in a situation when you can use these products, they're fresh on your mind. We close deals in the same way. It's a war of attrition. If you constantly follow up with a seller, you will eventually be the only person they're willing to sell to when that time comes. This is about situations and relationships. We've mainly talked tactics here, but I will dive more and more into strategy throughout the book. I just want you to know how much time or money you need to set aside to bring in high-quality leads. This is a business, not a hobby, so treat it like one.

When to Escalate

Beyond door knocking and cold-calling, there are other methods like direct mail, lead partnerships, and referrals, but the ideas behind all of these methods are essentially the same. It's about your time. It's about your budget. It's about creating a series of routes to find consistent leads. Rather than reiterate the same thing in multiple sections, I want to talk about the moment of escalation, meaning when you should take one process to the next. The key factors here are going to involve timing, price, motivation, and condition. This is the foundation of the four pillars for my team.

- **Timing**. "Are you interested in selling your house in the next sixty to ninety days?" This is a standard question we generally ask in the first call. We don't want to waste our time with people who aren't ever going to sell or will not want to sell for a year or so. If they're not interested in selling immediately, we will ask why there's a delay so we know if we should follow up in six months or not (and if they say to follow up in six months, we'll follow up in three to five months). This could be due to any number of reasons. Maybe they need to go through a house they inherited and there's some emotional reason they can't sell at that time. Maybe they're waiting on a job offer. It could be anything, but if they're not ready right away, their motivation and pain points are not high enough for us to negotiate. If they say no, ask them for a good time frame to follow up. If they say yes, move on to price.

- **Price**. How do you talk to people about price? I flat-out ask, "What are you trying to accomplish?" It's somewhat blunt, but it's less intrusive than asking, "What price are you looking for?" (which is what most people do). When you find out what they're trying to accomplish or walk away with, you have more room to negotiate, because there are more tools you can use. I also like to throw out multiple prices.

  Another version of this question is "In a perfect world, what price would you be looking for?" Even if I think the house is only worth $50,000 I might ask if they're looking for $1 million or $100,000, so I can feed them some bait to gauge a response. They'll likely say, "Not a million," and laugh, but then say the truth, like, "Not a million, but I saw other houses in the area selling for $75,000, so I want something around that." I don't worry about what number they say, it just changes my approach. It's all about fact-finding in the first conversation with a seller. Any number works, I just want to know what that number is; I want to know the barriers or limitations. I want my cold callers or my acquisition team to pull this number from the seller so I have an idea of what they're looking for before I hop on a call.

If you have a team, they should do this legwork for you. The same is true for meeting someone in person. Why drive to look at a property if there's not a price in mind? It doesn't mean I need to start to negotiate yet. It just means we need to have a conversation to see how serious the seller is about the potential deal. Since we're reaching out to unlisted sellers, they're often going to say, "I haven't thought much about it," or, "I need to talk to my wife/husband." Continue forward by saying, "Great. I'll give you a few days to talk it over and let's touch base next week." I want them to have their conversation about price before I spend my time on a pitch because I don't want that to be the issue as to why they make another delay. I flat-out tell them to have their price conversation before we meet in person or before our next call. Then we can have a more fruitful conversation. I want a yes or a no, not a delay.

- **Motivation**. Why are they interested in selling their house? I want to know the situation to know my next move, to reiterate the timeline, and to see their sense of urgency. I also want to know why they're willing to sell to a cash buyer rather than work with a Realtor or sell FSBO (for sale by owner). Maybe they want to avoid the Realtor cost. Maybe they don't want the hassle. I bring up time a lot, so much so they will sometimes ask, "Why do you ask so much about time frame?" One reason is that I can use this to deflect away from price, but also because I don't want to give the seller my price. I want to hear their price first so I know how to respond. Some buyers like to give a soft pitch in terms of price, but this is not my style. I answer the timeline question by saying, "I can only buy so many houses, and if your timeline is nine months away, I'm going to put you on the back burner and revisit this house later."

- **Condition**. Finally, I ask about the condition of the home. I don't care about the condition, but I want to see what the seller thinks about the property. You may hear a seller who owns a house from the 1960s say, "It's original but it's in great shape." I mean, okay, but it's still sixty years old so it's outdated to say the least. Again, I want to hear what they think of the house. I need a gauge of their situation. I need to find out if there's a tenant in the property or if they live in the property and if there's a situation of escrow before someone can move out. These all alter the timeline and potentially the price of the house. I may need to factor in cleaning costs if there's a hoarder situation because I want to solve all of their problems in order to close the deal. Then we talk about the physical condition of the home in more detail.

The general escalation flow involves a cold caller discussing timing, price, motivation, and condition of the home. This first call confirms the seller's name, the address, the callback number, an email, whether they're working with a Realtor or not, the year the house was built, how long they've had the property, and the occupancy status, then answers questions like roof condition, HVAC condition, size, square footage, time frame, motivation to sell, and asking price. Some of this can be found online, but you want to confirm as much as possible because online data is not always correct. It sounds like a lot, but a VA can handle all of this in a five- to ten-minute phone call. Once this has been done, a cold lead can become a warm lead or it can move to another section of the pipeline. Warm leads are then sent to me or another negotiator on the team when the cold caller makes an appointment.

Finally, it's time to negotiate. I'll discuss this more in Chapter 9, but essentially the goal is to see if you are a fit for the seller. Once the cold caller has done all this legwork, it's a warm lead. I don't care about price (yet); it's more about choosing my next strategy. Once a name enters my customer relationship management program (CRM), it's a warm lead I can focus on. Early on, I handled all of these calls, but now that I'm at a scaled position, my team sets appointments and tries to lock up these negotiations over the phone. I really only step in when a situation is particularly difficult or unique. I like these situations. I like difficult conversations as long as I know there's a possibility of closing the deal. I don't want to deal with cold calls that aren't serious, but I will solve someone's problem by buying a property if I can find a reasonable or creative solution to that problem.

Recently, a warm lead went through our process until it got to me, but I had to say, "Sounds like you're not ready. Sounds like you need a week or two to think this over, so why don't I give you my price in a week once you've gone through everything else?" This seller was talking to a few different wholesalers, so the reason I wanted to wait a week is because I knew my price might change in a week. I knew the seller's sense of urgency would change after they went through all these other offers. As a learning exercise, I also sent my recording over to my team so they knew how to improve on asking the right questions. This was an appointment that shouldn't have been booked yet, but it's a learning experience and the goal is to get better over time. The way you know you're getting better is by tracking your KPIs and reestablishing your goals month by month and quarter by quarter.

INVESTOR STORY
Jordan Fulmer—Creative Sub-To Deals
"Don't throw away good leads . . ."

Jordan Fulmer lives in Huntsville, Alabama. He's been in real estate for about four years but is new to the sub-to community. One seller brought Jordan a deal not long after they met. The sellers loved the first creative deal so much they were open to doing another deal with Jordan and his wife.

The first acquisition was a sub-to, and Jordan sold it on a lease option. The second was a sub-to that he sold on a wholesale exit. He found the first deal doing direct mail. Direct mail can be expensive depending on the market. In medium markets, you can get some good leads for less money. But in Phoenix, you might spend $10,000 on one good lead. Seeing that direct mail come back means the property is vacant; most people ignore that, but it's great news. You just need to use a program to skip-trace the number. You know that everyone else is tossing those returned envelopes and literally throwing away good leads.

Some of Jordan's postcards bounced back. He skip-traced the returned postcards and found the phone number of the seller in the first property. He knew no one else was able to reach the seller, so it could be a good lead.

After the skip trace, Jordan called and the woman was happy to sell the house. They set up a time to talk through the deal and he learned that she had just gotten married. When she got married, she moved, and this house was mostly vacant. Her daughter was supposed to live in it and fix it up, but that didn't happen, and now the owner and her husband were carrying two payments. The property needed about $32,000 of work to sell.

The other good news is that this seller hadn't gotten any other offers (that they knew about because of the vacant property). When Jordan made an offer, he was the only contender other than a neighbor who had asked about it. Jordan doesn't see negotiating as a bare-knuckle problem. He's open on the phone about how he uses cash and how he also uses creative finance to close and sometimes pay more.

Jordan offered sub-to with a little bit of cash as one option, and then a wrap, which meant the seller would get a higher price overall but less up front, as a second. She wanted the cash up front, so she took the first deal. The inspection led to some issues, so Jordan ended up giving the seller $5,000 in addition to the sub-to deal, which was around $92,000 in total. In this case, the $5,000 came out of pocket, but there are countless ways to connect with people in the community who would be able to lend a smaller amount of money like this as private money. With the wrap, the PITI was $950 per month and Jordan leased it out for $1,350, so he made about $400 cash flow. He also got a $7,500 option fee from the lease buyer and eventually sold the house for $170,000 after being in for about $125,000 total.

However, appreciation is so crazy that the house is likely worth over $270,000, so they undersold it, which is why I no longer do lease options. But in the beginning, when you don't want to manage a property, lease options make sense.

Regardless, the seller liked the deal so much that she brought Jordan another house. It was even easier to sell the second house wholesale to other buyers in the area. Currently, to replace his income, Jordan's model involved a wholesale deal every month and then working to scale with rentals and other exit strategies. In the end, you have to think about your overall goals and realign to meet those goals. I would recommend wholesaling three to four properties a month and keeping one, so you make money now and later. Meanwhile, you have to keep your living expenses the same.

When he started in real estate, Jordan's first deal was a traditional deal, which meant he had to pay about 20 percent down, which could be $25,000 or $30,000. This alone made him move toward creative finance because he couldn't do other deals like this one and make it work long-term. It's too expensive. With creative finance, he could put down a few thousand dollars and then use any money he needed on repairs and those sorts of things.

KEY TAKEAWAY | Figure out marketing methods that no one else is doing and never throw away good leads or avoid doing the hard work; that's where the riches can be found.

CHAPTER 8

How Do I Know If It's a Deal?

"The wings don't make you fly and the crown don't make you king."

—LUPE FIASCO, "GOLD WATCH"

Most real estate books talk about "motivated sellers," but there's always more to it than that. If they answer the phone, they're somewhat of a motivated seller—tired landlords have gotten lots of these calls over the years and are used to ignoring unknown calls—but that doesn't mean they're open to selling you their property just because you managed to get them on the phone. You have to find a motivated seller and then ask the right questions. It's a dance. It's dating. It's this connection you must build over a handful of phone calls based on their situation and what you can do for them. That's why they call it relationship building. Let's go over some of the common reasons a seller might be willing to work with you in the first place.

Generally, we find unlisted deals, but occasionally we will find deals on the MLS that work out for us. They have keywords like "cash only" or "property sold as is" or "bring all offers" or "no reasonable offer refused" right there in the listing. If you're brand-new to real estate and don't have much time or money to acquire leads, you can look for these types of listings, but it's rarer to find MLS listings, so these aren't great for long-term sustainability.

When you do get on the phone with the seller, you will discover all sorts of situations. The seller could be:

- Moving out of the area.
- Dealing with a life-changing moment, like the death of a loved one or a divorce.
- A tired landlord and the property has been sitting vacant or they just no longer want to deal with the maintenance.
- Wanting to downsize or move to a warmer climate.
- Just not wanting to do all of the work required to make the home livable or rentable.
- Threatened with a foreclosure.
- Wanting to get rid of a property they inherited and don't want.
- Trying to invest elsewhere.

The list goes on and on, but your job is to figure out why they want to sell, and then see if you are the right buyer or can find the right buyer to help their situation. Why would a seller want to sell with seller finance? That's the big question and it's something that confuses wholesalers, cash buyers, and most people who focus on traditional real estate exchanges. But here's my question: Why would a seller sell you a house for 60 cents on the dollar? To me, that makes less sense than a seller wanting 100 percent or 120 percent of the value of their home. I use the F-150 story I mentioned in Chapter 2 time and time again to help explain seller finance in a simple, logical way.

The seller says, "I don't understand what seller finance is. I don't know what that means." And I say, "You're going to be the bank." And they respond, "I don't comprehend that, I'm not a real estate investor, Pace. What are you talking about?" I continue, "Okay, let me tell you about my infamous F-150.

"I was a contractor for a long time and we had this F-150 in our fleet. And this F-150 hit 320,000 miles and it came time that we needed to sell it and get something different, because it was starting to have little issues here and there and it would cause problems on job sites.

"I go on Kelley Blue Book—it tells you the value, it's like the Zillow for cars, basically. I check Kelley Blue Book and I'm like, 'What the heck, my truck is only worth $5,000? Screw that.'"

I tell the seller, "I did essentially what you did. I put it on Craigslist for $10,000—an insane amount of money, but what I thought it was worth. Do you think I got $10,000?"

They say, "No, you probably got an offer at $7,500."

"Nope! I didn't even get a phone call," I replied. "For three months I tried to sell this truck for more than anybody was willing to pay for it, because everyone else has access to Kelley Blue Book too. One day, my wife came into my office, touched me on the shoulder, and said, 'Hey, sweetheart, is there any way we can get that stupid truck out of the driveway?' I was like, 'What do you want me to do? The truck is worth more than $5,000 to me, and if I put it on Craigslist for $5,000, then I'm probably going to get lowballed at $3,500. And I'm just not willing to sell it for that.'"

I say to the seller, "Does that make sense? You're kind of in that situation right now with your house. You are getting people lowballing you and it's just not worth it for you." They agree.

"My wife said, 'Pace, you're the creative finance guy, why don't you put it on Craigslist and tell them that you'll take smaller payments for the $10,000 instead of a lump sum?' And I thought, 'Oh my gosh, where were you three months ago, sweetheart? You're a genius!' Sometimes it takes a second pair of eyes to point out what's right in front of your face. I go back to Craigslist and I change on thing: 'F-150, will take payments.'"

Continuing my story to the seller, I say, "Do you think I sold that truck for $10,000?"

"Oh, probably," they reply.

"I had to turn my Craigslist ad off within forty-five minutes. I was overwhelmed with calls. I ended up selling it for $12,500 because I gave somebody the ability to give me payments. That's what we're doing here," I continue.

"If you're willing to take payments for your home, I'm willing to pay more than anybody else. But your terms have to make sense for me. I give you the price you want, you give me the terms I need."

I've used that story multiple times with sellers. If nothing else, it helps continue the conversation, because most people haven't heard of seller financing or they haven't heard of subject-to or the other methods discussed in this book. Like all rational people, sellers need information to make an informed decision. That's your job—to educate. For the most part, these initial negotiations are not about convincing someone to sell. They're about educating someone. Then you can start to overcome objections and get to the real situation the seller has. As an investor, your job is to present information and solve problems. A lot of times, you're also going against the norm, but it's more beneficial for the seller.

Let's say the seller is being told not to do seller finance by their lender, their financial advisor, and their real estate agent. Why? All three of those people benefit from the seller using traditional finance. They want their combined 11 percent or whatever bogus number they think it's worth to help someone sell a house. They say the transaction can't be done. When you get the chance to talk directly to the seller, you can present information in an accurate manner, let them know their real options, and provide a type of value no one else can match. I go over seller objections more in Chapter 9, but right now I want to talk about seller situations.

Asking Better Questions

When investors have problems with their creative finance deals, the biggest problem I see is that they haven't asked enough questions of their seller. They haven't obtained enough information to even figure out what is going on. They're more focused on trying to close the deal than they are on figuring out what the situation is for the seller. A lot of times, I will tell investors that I don't have enough information to answer their questions because they didn't gather enough information. They didn't connect with the seller. They didn't put in the groundwork to build that rapport and create that relationship in order to build trust. After you build that initial foundation, you can then start talking about numbers and closing the deal.

When you ask the right questions, it can change your perspective on the deal, because you can always find out more information about the seller. Here's an example: I got on the phone with a seller named Kathy and I asked these follow-up questions myself. Kathy began the call with a question: "What do you have to tell me?"

I responded, "I don't have anything to tell you, but I do have a couple things to ask you. I've got some missing notes and I just had a couple questions for you."

Most people only ask about the house. They want to confirm what they see on Zillow or wherever they're gathering their information. They want to confirm things like the year built, whether or not the seller is working with a Realtor, occupancy status, condition, asking price, and the motivation to sell. Sometimes the seller will give you all this information on the first call. Sometimes they won't. People are naturally a little closed off, especially when talking to a stranger on the phone. The longer you talk, the more information you are likely to gather. Initially they will often give reasons of motivation like "willing to sell if the price is right" or "tired of managing the property" or "getting older and tired of maintenance." But other times they don't necessarily know their own reason or they're shy about admitting it, so you have to dig deeper.

Kathy told me she wanted $150,000 for a property that she inherited from her parents. I needed to ask her if she just wanted that money to pay off the existing loan. I asked, "Is that exactly what you owe on the house?" She told me she had a little more money saved up and needed $150,000 to close the deal. This is traditional financing. This is how most people think about real estate. But that's not the deal that made sense for me. I told her, "I've got an idea. If I'm going to buy this house, I'm not going to buy it with cash; I'm going to get a loan from a bank. I buy a lot of houses, so if I bought all my houses with cash, I'd have to be the son of Bill Gates or something," I joked. "I have to get loans on houses. What happens is I get a loan from a bank to pay off a loan from your parents' bank. Essentially, the only people who make money in that transaction are both the banks. Instead, would you be willing for me to take over the payments on your parents' house and give you some cash on top of that?"

Her response was simply no. But then she added, "It's my family home and it's going to be handed down in my family. I don't want anybody else on the property." This is when I found out what the initial communication with the acquisition manager was about. Kathy wanted to keep this house. She wanted to sell a different house that she owned in another state in order to take ownership of her parents' former house. She needed to sell the other house to make some money to buy the first house and pay off that mortgage. She then told me she owned several properties that she inherited from the death of her sister. She also said she was upside-down in these deals and she wouldn't earn much on them. I asked her, "If you just want to buy your parents' house, why don't you take over the loan payments?" Then she told me the fundamental missing piece.

"It's not a loan, it's a reverse mortgage. When the mortgager dies, the loan has to be paid back or you lose the property. I'm on retirement pay; my house in Florida is paid for, but it's not in a condition where I can make what I need to make selling it. I'm just trying to figure out how I can get this house. It's the only thing I've got from my parents and I want to keep it. They worked their whole lives for it."

Not only did this clarify the issue for me, but it allowed for the seller to open up and connect on an emotional level. She wanted the house. She wanted everything in it. If I wanted to deal with her, I needed to focus on the house in Florida and figure out how to help her close on this reverse mortgage issue. "I knew when I bought it that Tallahassee would expand outward. It's a capital city. It's a college town. That property is going to keep going up," she told me. "I lost my baby sister. I lost my nephew. I lost my brother. I lost my mother. I lost my father. I've been here taking care of all of them, so I couldn't tend to my needs, take care of my properties and my investments. I've lost everybody," she said.

Do you think she told this story to everybody who called her or do you think she only told it to those willing to listen to her?

"Where would all of these people be without you?"

"I don't know," she said.

She's the linchpin of her family. She's made good investments, but because of these situations with different family members, she was unable to take care of herself. Now we can talk about the house in Florida. "Do you think the house in Florida is a good deal at $150,000?" She disclosed that the house had water damage, so it would either need to be renovated or torn down and rebuilt. She also said the house was vacant and she had had some offers, but she'd rather let the house fall down than lose money on the deal since the value of the land would continue to go up. She also owned some mobile homes but didn't want to sell those, as these properties would cash flow in her immediate future.

Now what do we do? Is the house in Florida worth $150,000? Is there something I can do to help Kathy keep her parents' house and buy this deal in Florida? At this point, I thought I knew everything, so I reached back out to the acquisition person who had seen this house in Florida and we started to discuss the deal. This deal ended up not working out for us, because you have to do a short sale or fix-and-flip in a reverse mortgage situation, which doesn't fit my buy box for Florida. But the real reason this didn't work wasn't the reverse mortgage. It was that Kathy had an emotional affinity for the property I would've wanted to buy. She didn't want someone else's name on the deed, so a creative deal didn't work. It takes time to get this information. You need all of the information to make sure a deal fits your buy box. It's tough to lose a deal, but that's the game. And, for me, it either fits my buy box or it's a pass.

Problem-Solving

When we use cold callers and door knockers, the goal is always to set an appointment. With a seller appointment, I can get face-to-face with a seller and explain how subject-to can solve problems unlike any other method they've heard before. More often than not, the seller has already been pitched half a dozen times and doesn't want to take a lowball offer, but they also don't want to deal with a Realtor. Depending on their situation, sellers often find themselves between a rock and a hard place. It's here that we can provide a solution that works out for everyone.

Here's an example of what that looks like. Recently, after my acquisition team set up an appointment, I met a seller, Anthony, in his home and we spoke at his coffee table about his hesitancy. My goal was to get additional information, build rapport, and work on pitching a subject-to deal. "I've heard from many friends and family members that I should get whatever I can get and move on. Then, two years later, I can start over," said the seller. "Before I bought this house, my credit was bad, but I paid off my other debts and bought this house. It was time to be a grown-up, so that's what we did. But then when we bought the house, I lost my job, and we got into more financial difficulties. I was making $100,000 a year. But now I'm looking for jobs and they're saying I'm overqualified and no one will hire me. It started snowballing. Bills got past due. It's funny, because we got a modification, but we didn't use it because we filed for bankruptcy. We put every debt in one bill and just paid it, but it was a large bill. We were paying $2,400 when my mortgage was only $1,400 and we did that for months."

Anthony shared with me that he called his attorney and tried to work out a better deal to pay down his debt. He even met with a trustee, but he was essentially in foreclosure. That's how my team met Anthony. We had called him, texted him, sent ringless voice mails, and then finally knocked on his door. He told us he had already spoken to other investors, who lost interest after they learned he didn't have any equity in the property. At this point, he didn't think we could help him either. All of these wholesalers he had spoken to had offered him small amounts of money, but we told him we could leave his mortgage in place, give him some money to walk away, and take that huge burden off his shoulders. If he would let us, we could solve his problem.

For my meeting with Anthony, I sat down and said, "Catch me up to speed with everything." This is for the seller to present their information to me so I can figure out whether I can help them. Even if it's not a perfect scenario, I come in like a detective and want to hear the story again. This makes the seller repeat the story and possibly reveal more information. It's also possible my team got something wrong or missed something as they've likely talked in person and on the phone at various times, or that there's new information to discuss. It's also different talking to someone in person than on the phone. It's possible the seller says the exact opposite of what they told my team simply because they were putting up walls during a phone conversation; those walls tend to come down when you're face-to-face with a person.

Anthony had gone to the bank to get a loan modification and he had worked with a Realtor before. However, they had already scheduled an auction date. "There have been a lot of people calling me and leaving cards on my door. This one guy looked at the house and I told him what I wanted. He had the paperwork. I was this close to signing it, but my wife was at work and the guy needed her signature too. I called her, said we can get what we want, but we need to sign today. My wife told me to wait and she called the mortgage company. My wife said she didn't want to do the deal. The guy offered me more than what I wanted, but we weren't ready to sell."

I told him my position and provided more information than usual since he was already versed in real estate terminology. "You don't have to have good credit to buy a house. You think as a traditional homeowner that you have to have good credit and your bankruptcy is going to keep you from buying a house. I buy twelve houses a month utilizing creative structuring that doesn't require pulling my credit or pulling a loan," I told him. He nodded along, but then asked if I had backing. "No. I want to teach you my methods whether or not I buy your house. This will change your entire financial life."

The reason I was telling him this is because I didn't want him worried about not being able to buy a house in the future. I wanted to calm his nerves. I wanted to teach him how to use creative finance just so he knew it was an option for his seemingly uncertain future. I listened to him so I could highlight the things that he had an emotional response to. In this case, it was about being able to buy another house and get his life back on track. The other positive about this is that when you show up as someone who can help, you don't have to worry about bringing up sensitive information. It's all relative in order to truly help and serve someone.

"The transaction is called subject-to. Has anyone ever talked to you about that?" He shook his head. "Subject-to means you can give the house to someone else, but you keep the debt. You've got a mortgage in place. How far in arrears are you?" He was about $17,500 in arrears. "Okay, that means I can pay your bank $17,500 and then buy your house from you and get you out of foreclosure. I can pay closing costs, and then I'm the new owner and I never had to get a loan. We don't call the mortgage company. I own the title, but the debt is still in your name. Even my personal house, where I have a 3.25 percent interest rate, I bought in a similar way We do this all the time."

It was about this time when he asked one of the six most common questions.

The Six Questions Sellers Ask

The wheels were turning for Anthony and this was all starting to make sense. "It doesn't matter if you have two loans. It matters if you're responsible for those loans," I explained.

Then, he asked a common question (let's call this Question One): "What happens if you stop payment and the loan is still in my name?" It's a valid question.

"That would be the best thing that could happen to you. You would get the house back, even after I caught you up in arrears, paid closing costs, and put some cash in your pocket. Why do you care if I stop paying? You made $20,000 or $30,000." He asked the question again, so I gave a clearer answer. "What we do is sign a piece of paper called a performance deed. If I don't perform or I'm thirty days behind, you automatically get the deed back. And we're not talking six months' back payment. We're only talking about thirty days. Other guys who do this force foreclosure, but I don't want you to worry about that, so that's why we do a performance deed through a title company. It's held at title, signed by both parties. You wouldn't have to fight me. The title company would just give you the house back."

I overcame his first objection, but then I wanted to take him through the next five most common questions, so I could solve those problems before they even came up. "Sellers always ask what happens if I miss a payment. Then they ask me if this is legal. Yes, it's legal. Title companies all over the country do this all the time. I've got hours of this on YouTube if you want to learn more about it, plus you can talk to my title company.

"Question Number Three: People ask me what happens if the market crashes, and now I own a property where I owe $247,000 but the market says the house is now only worth $190,000. People ask, 'What happens if 2008 happens again?' But I don't buy the house based on the value of the house. I buy the house based on the cash flow it represents. I underwrite deals. If your mortgage is $1,500 but you don't have a homeowner association (HOA), let's say you can rent this house out for $2,000 or so. I can cash flow this property for $350 a month after I pay repairs and maintenance and such. Technically, you could do that, but you would have to catch up on arrears first.

"It's an opportunity for you," I continued. "I can pay the arrears, put some money in your pocket, and create cash flow for myself. It's not huge. Most properties I can cash flow $500–$700 per month. We do group homes. Assisted living. Airbnbs. But this house would be a rental. For me, I don't have to get a traditional mortgage. I ran out of the ability to get a traditional mortgage a hundred houses ago. You can only get thirteen mortgages in your name in the traditional manner, so I had to find creative ways to buy houses." I then told him I would pay more than he wanted for the house, as long as I could structure it out to make cash flow. "The thing about 2008 is that even though the market crashed, the rental rates went up. The rental rates in this country haven't gone down in, like, thirty years."

"Question Number Four is: 'What if you die or get abducted by aliens or something?' Again, the answer is the performance deed.

That's as good as cash in your pocket. You'd get the house back, caught up, with money in your pocket, and I'd put a little money into a renovation. Worst-case scenario, you'd get it back within one day of me not performing." This is usually the part where I start telling third-party stories so they can see I've done this before and do this regularly, and that there's an answer to every concern. I also want to confirm that other people have agreed to these terms or similar terms. Third-party stories and mirroring are essential to build rapport. They are like social proof before the advent of social media.

For this conversation, I was also writing down all the numbers on a sheet of paper so everything was clear and transparent. "I had another seller who was way behind. They were about $40,000 behind, so we put about $10,000 in their pocket. The husband was just ready to get out of the deal so he could get another house. He wanted to get rid of this burden and provide another solution. His wife was anxious," I said, to show it mirrored Anthony's situation. "She said, 'You're telling me that if I scare your renters off, I get the house back?' I said yes, but that won't happen, because one vacant house is not a big deal. We have hundreds of houses. We would just lower the rent. But, just in case, for your peace of mind, you have the performance deed."

"Question Five is: 'Can I buy the house back from you?' Rarely is the answer no, but most people don't want it back when the time comes," I told him.

"And Question Six is: 'If you buy the house, can I stay in the house and rent it from you?' The answer is also no, but it's because the seller was used to paying, say, $1,500, but now the rent is $2,000. Sellers don't want to pay more, and it's also no longer their house." I want to be clear about everything up front. I want to tell the seller this before it's an emotional point. "We had a guy do this and he quickly got upset that he was paying more money and didn't own the house. It's emotional. It's a weird thing." Anthony confirmed he had asked the previous investor many of the same questions. The fun part of this business is getting good enough to learn these ins and outs. You start to be able to read the situations and close like crazy. Plus, you get to help people solve their problems.

I continued, "What I would rather do is teach you how to buy a house subject-to. Millions of people go through foreclosures like this. People feel isolated, but it happens all the time. What I would rather do than have you rent a place is help you buy a place. You don't have to get qualified." Giving him this option helped him take this journey with me. I gave him the ability to buy another house. I gave him a way out. I gave him the option of being a provider for his family again, despite this setback. "We get houses with similar interest rates. You don't have to qualify. You don't have to get a loan."

Finally, he said, "Why have I never heard of this before!?"

I told him, "Because the only people educating homeowners are real estate agents and all they do is put a sign in the yard. But with subject-to and creative finance, I don't need marketing because I'm providing solutions. If you provide a solution that nobody else is doing, you don't need to advertise." Anthony agreed and then I later explained everything to his wife. On the second appointment we closed the deal.

Comping and Underwriting

Have you ever heard the terms "comping" or "underwriting?" Maybe you've heard them used interchangeably, but they're two different methods. Comping is for wholesalers and fix-and-flippers, while underwriting is for creative finance investors. Comping is about finding the value of the property. Underwriting is about finding the strategy in terms of what tools to use to close on the deal. You might comp a property to discover the seller wants way too much money, which means you take that comp and move it to the underwriting strategy. From your point of view, this is about changing your perspective on the deal. They want too much money to make a cash offer, so how can we create an offer on terms that will work? Knowing that the seller wants $200,000 for a $200,000 house, there may be a strategy better than cash that can still make the deal work. Without comping and underwriting the property, you won't be able to negotiate.

Here's the question: Is this a deal or is this not a deal? The way to figure out the answer starts with comping. Most investors will only buy a property where comps are available. "Comps" means comparable properties. I want to share some appraisal rules from my good friend Jamil Damji. Jamil would tell you, "Understanding value is the foundation of your real estate career." When I first started in this business, I met Jamil as a KeyGlee dispo agent, meaning he was part of the KeyGlee real estate investment team. Jamil credits his initial success in the business with being able to understand what a property is worth. Once you know what a property is worth, you will know whether or not you have a deal. Jamil has also said, "The dream-killer of wholesalers is canceling their first deal they get under contract. They spend this time cold-calling, talking to people, sending text messages . . . but they don't understand what a property is actually worth. When you don't know what a property is worth, you don't know what to offer, you lock up deals too high, you don't find a buyer, and you don't get paid." Investors want to avoid these dream killers. In order to do so, we use specific appraisal rules and we adjust them over time as we learn more and more.

Jamil spent nine months creating his rules by working with hundreds of appraisers and going to appraisal school. Early in my career, I would send properties to Jamil and ask him if they made sense and what numbers I should offer. Using his rules, Jamil knew what to tell me and eventually taught me how to comp and how to find the ARV, or after-repair value. Every deal is dependent on these rules. If a deal didn't make sense or Jamil said the seller wanted too much, I had to walk away from the deal. Today, I would just shift to creative finance and try to make it work.

When you are comping a property, your potential deal is what's known as the subject property. Everything else that mirrors that deal is known as a comp. You need to make sure your comp and your subject property are as similar as possible. Everyone does gymnastics to find a comp that looks good but is ultimately not usable. We fall in love with a deal and think we can talk a buyer into buying it. But when you start to break these rules, you're lying to yourself. This is no way to close deals. Finding these comps is the only way to become the best in your market. In busy areas, there are going to be more comps than in less busy areas. In Phoenix, where I do deals, I make sure my subject property is in the same subdivision as my comps. This makes it a true comp. In less-busy areas, you're going to have to stretch your comping locations out to find similar deals, and then it's less certain whether they're a true comp. If you have a property in Subdivision 1, you need to comp in Subdivision 1. A comp in Subdivision 3 might have been built a decade later. It's not the same.

You also can't compare across any major roads. Appraisers will only cross a major road when there are no comps available in that subdivision, but then it's not a true comp. It is not uncommon, especially in places like Houston, to have a subdivision of older $200,000 houses right across a major road from a subdivision of newer million-dollar homes. It's better to even use a comp that's two years old compared to leaving your subdivision to find a comp that fits the narrative you're trying to create. You also need to find a comp constructed within five years of the subject property.

Once you confirm the subdivision, you need to make sure the sizes of the properties are within 200 square feet of each other. Once you go above a 400-square-foot difference, your dollar per square foot tends to be incorrect. A lot of new wholesalers look for a comp for a 1,000-square-foot house and find a 2,000-square-foot property. These dollar-per-square-foot amounts are not the same. Beyond square footage, you then need to compare property type. If your subject property is a single-story rancher, your comp needs to be a single-story rancher. If your subject property is a two-story house, you need to comp a two-story house. If your property is in a historic district, your comp needs to be in a historic district.

A subject property and its comp must also share certain attributes that change property values. Adding a bedroom will give you another $10,000–$25,000. Adding a bathroom will give you another $10,000–$25,000. In my area, adding a pool will give you another $10,000–$25,000 (but pools don't always close deals and some buyers see them as a liability). Adding a garage will give you another $10,000. Adding a carport will give you another $10,000.

Sometimes certain features subtract value from a property. If a property sits on a major road or is next to commercial property, this proximity could subtract at least $10,000–$20,000 from the appraisal value. If the house is next to a location that would stigmatize it, such as a cemetery, this can cause a major devaluation (as in, you might want to walk away or understand this will be a hard sell). Then there are features you assume would add a lot of value, such as a basement or guesthouse, but the value of these features' square footage is only assessed at about 50 percent of the price per square foot for the rest of the house.

Here's how important it is to comp correctly: When I see someone justify a horrible comp in an email, I unfollow their buyer's list (this means I literally unsubscribe from the emails they send to potential buyers). They lose all credibility with me. I might give a new whole-saler a chance and I'm happy to walk investors through the dos and don'ts. Justifying a bad comp is just lying to yourself and it makes you lose credibility since you're out there trying to pitch false deals. It drives me crazy how poorly some wholesalers comp. They just reach too far and it's nonsense. I see those same wholesalers complaining, "Why can't I sell my deals? Wholesaling is so hard. I lock up seven deals but only close one; must be my buyer's list." It's not their buyer's list. It's bad comping. If you believe in giving people value as a service, it's your job to comp correctly. I'll ask a newbie to justify their number so I can help them find a true one, but you can't justify bad numbers. That's not how it works.

This stuff isn't sexy, but it's important. You need to take time and practice comping deals until you start to naturally see the true comps. If you're brand-new to the business, it's a good idea to partner with someone who knows how to comp. That's exactly what I did and it helped me bypass years of scratching my head. See how they do it. See what they do and what they don't do. Working with someone who quickly understands how to comp will make you able to comp quickly. Jamil and I can comp a property in thirty seconds, but it takes practice. You get faster and faster and better and better the more you do it. For more details, Jamil also has a YouTube series called "Straight Outta Compin'" where he breaks all of this down even further.

COMPING TOOLS

For comping, a lot of people use sites like Zillow, but I prefer to use multiple tools. I always want the best comping tools available with the most up-to-date information. Currently, we use the BatchLeads suite of products but we're always looking for new comping tools. You can check my YouTube channel to see what product we're currently using.

Another favorite is the BiggerPockets rent estimator (www.bigger pockets.com/insights/property-searches/new), where you can instantly get accurate rental pricing for any property, thanks to their proprietary, investor-focused data. We use several platforms and apps for list building and a number of other things, but comping is also one of the key features. The way we start is by entering an address into one of the websites. Inside these programs, you can see everything you need to properly comp. You can see square footage, bedrooms, bathrooms, year built, heating type, AC type, and a number of other items. When we do cold calls, we like to confirm these numbers, because a seller could have added a bathroom or done any number of other upgrades that wouldn't be in the initial data. Find the tool you like the most; it's a personal preference. But also use other tools because when you do talk to sellers, they're likely just using Zillow and whatever algorithm currently makes up the "Zestimate" for a given home. If you also check Zillow or whatever is most common in your area, you may already know their number to get started on the negotiation.

When you're comping a property, you need to know the sale price on the properties you are using as comparisons for your subject property. But to accomplish this, you need to know if you are in a disclosure or nondisclosure state. I live in Arizona, which is a disclosure state. This means that when a property or house is sold, the price it was sold for is released to the public and is visible on third-party sites like Zillow. However, in nondisclosure states, like Texas, when a home is sold, the sale price is not disclosed and the "price" you see on

Zillow is just the price that Zillow estimates the house sold for. You can look at the price history on some sites like Zillow and Redfin to see the last price the house was listed for to get a ballpark idea of the sale price. But in nondisclosure states, the only way to get an accurate sold price is to get access to the MLS (usually by becoming an agent) or through a third-party program.

When you're looking at comps, you need to make sure you're getting as close as possible by using the best information available. I personally like to think of comping as a three-tier system. In Tier 1, you have the date sold and the distance from the subject property. It is extremely important to understand the date sold. Looking at a property sold four years ago is not relevant because there was a different economy four years ago and the location has changed in that time. A lot can happen in four years. Generally, you want to find a comp that's from fewer than six months ago. This isn't always available, but it's the goal. I like to find the same type of property that sold in the last three months. For me, to sell as a wholesaler, I can sell this to a fix-and-flipper, but that person is going to have to get someone to appraise the property. This will take another three months, so that creates its own six-month time frame just to do the deal. The appraiser can't go back more than six months without having permission from their superior. Likewise, distance is critical. Stay within the same subdivision or one-mile radius. Don't pull comps from a gated community if you're buying in a non-gated community. The same is true for properties with and without a view and other attributes considered luxuries. Comps should be comparable. That's the whole point.

In Tier 2, we've got things like interior square footage, parking, year built, bed and bath count, and general condition. The condition of the property can perhaps be delineated with a construction estimate, but you can't change the other attributes. To change things in Tier 2 in order to increase the resale value can take a lot of work. This might mean turning a spare room into a bedroom or adding a bathroom.

In Tier 3, we've got proximity to roads, lot size, pool, and build type. For the longest time, I didn't think proximity to roads mattered as much as it did, but it's crucial. It's a significant issue. As a fix-and-flipper, I've bought properties on busy roads and considered a 10 percent discount, but in reality it's more like a 25 percent discount. It took me forever to find a buyer for those properties. The same is true for funky lot sizes or lot locations. If you have to drive around the alley to park your car every time, it may stop a large percentage of buyers from even looking at the property. With pools, something to think about is that a $30,000 swimming pool doesn't mean you get a $30,000 bonus credit added to the appraisal. In my area, you may only get $10,000 or $12,000 max for having a swimming pool. In some cases, you'll lose money. Finally, there's build type. You can't compare a manufactured home to a single-level stick-built house. You can't compare a condo to a mansion. Build type matters.

You've done your comps; now what? Is it a deal or not? With comping, you're trying to find both the current value and the ARV. If you've ever heard the phrase "as is," this refers to the current value. A lot of times when you talk to sellers, they're going to comp their house with a completely repaired house on Zillow. In the real world, this doesn't work. If they haven't made changes in ten years or need a new roof, a completely remodeled house with a new roof is going to be worth more. The house can be fixed up to be worth the same or more, but it's not automatically worth the same amount. In an as-is condition, add up the cost to replace things like bad carpet, old cabinets, or other less-than-ideal qualities. Use that data to determine the data you need. When you know the ARV, you subtract everything that's missing and that determines your as-is value or current value.

The way that a homeowner sees the value of their house is vastly different from the value that an investor would place on their house. An investor looks at the numbers associated with a property, like their bottom line, costs, cash flow, etc. A homeowner, especially one who is not a real estate investor, has a lot of emotions wrapped up in their house and they believe their house is their biggest asset. They also hear what other people in their town have sold their houses for and assume their own house will sell for the same. Homeowners don't think about the fact that the house they heard about was built five years ago and is completely remodeled and up to date, but their home was built in 1970 and hasn't had a lot of updates since then. When you throw in the fact that these homeowners are looking online at computer-generated estimates, like Zillow's Zestimate, this all leads to a situation where a homeowner's expectation of how much they can sell their house for is often much higher than what an investor can pay for it. The same is true for what a mortgage appraiser would appraise the house for.

A lot of novice investors will send me deals where all they've done is some auto-comping—they've just checked the Zestimate online. Auto-comping is important and it's a good way to get a general sense or gut check of the value, but you have to put in the work to figure out the real information to find out whether or not you have a deal. You want to do this before you send the deal to someone else. Realtor and Zillow provide auto-comp numbers on nearly every home they include, whether or not it's on the market. But these mega lists don't know everything. They're just algorithms. That's why you have to talk to sellers, do your homework, and figure out the real numbers.

A more manual approach will better help you understand the market. You have to manually comp in order to be a ninja in real estate. Use your brain, go through the data, and get better over time. We need tools like the MLS, BatchLeads, PropStream, Zillow, Realtor, and so on, but only to gather information to come up with our own numbers. Most people use Zillow because they don't have access to the MLS, but this depends where you are in your business and what you can afford to spend per month on programs like these. Either way, you need to gather all of the crucial information to make an educated decision to find a deal.

To reiterate, with manual comping, you want to:
- Know your subject property.
- Find the ARV comp and how much it sold for.
- Adjust for differences.
- Confirm the ARV comp through other recent solds.
- Confirm with pending and under-contract comps.
- Confirm with active comps.

A special note on properties in pending status on the MLS. When you comp a pending property, this might not be the correct number. You will see a house pending for $250,000, but then the actual sold price is only $200,000 because the pending price locks in before escrow closes and these programs don't always have the correct amount. Pending prices are helpful but can be incorrect in the end. Use everything in this chapter as a guide, but know that comping is something you can improve at over time and learn what works best in your area and with your buyers. Likewise, other players are often just using Zillow or Realtor, so use these tools to get into the mindset of your seller, your buyer, and the market in order to be able to negotiate the best deal for yourself.

UNDERWRITING DEALS

Is it a deal or is it a dud? With underwriting, we can determine whether or not a potential deal is actually a deal. This means figuring out the ARV, determining the wholesale maximum allowable offer (WMAO), and using the Sub-To Formula.

We've covered comps in great detail, so let's talk about the WMAO, or the MAO for short. When we are trying to figure out this comp, we use a four-step system.

1. First, we pull a full fix-and-flip formula and then subtract the wholesale fee.

2. Then we use a flat percentage fee minus the rehab and minus the wholesale fee.

3. Next, we use a multiplier for the monthly rent.

4. Finally, we figure out the flat percentage of the wholesale fee.

The BiggerPockets calculators (www.biggerpockets.com/calculators) are one of the best tools out there for deal analysis, and there are options for everything from rental properties to fix-and-flips. Understanding deal analysis is a little easier with examples, so let's use one to go over fix-and-flip numbers and wholesale numbers with an Airbnb analysis. This is how I make about $500,000 a year in passive income. In a subject-to deal in Atlanta, Georgia, we manifested a deal with a gentleman named Jamari. Jamari sent me a DM on Instagram.

I asked him to get me on the phone with the seller, and after a forty-five-minute call, I was able to have Jamari follow up with the seller every single week until the seller was ready to make a sale.

In this situation, the seller was a Realtor herself. She was going through a foreclosure with a property and didn't have the time or the energy to deal with the property herself. She was familiar with subject-to, so we didn't need to go into the weeds with the explanation; we just needed to figure out the numbers. The seller was behind $41,000, so I agreed to catch up those payments before I closed escrow. People new to creative finance worry about numbers like this because they don't have an extra $41,000 lying around to catch up arrears. In this case, a short sale might be the right answer. But let's say you can raise private money or use another way to catch up arrears and you want to focus on a long-term deal. Another option might be to refinance the loan. Again, the more you know, the more options you have to help sellers in foreclosure. A loan modification, in this case, can be added to the back of a mortgage. The main goal is to fix the seller's problem. In this case, I raised private capital, which I talk more about in Chapter 12.

Let's break down the numbers. In the beginning of this deal, I've got $41,000 going to arrears. I've got $10,000 going to the seller just to walk away, and I'm giving another $10,000 to Jamari for bringing me the deal. In this case, Jamari didn't even have to close. He just had to keep following up. After everything was said and done, he earned about $1,100 each of the nine times he followed up with the seller. What changed? Why was the seller suddenly willing to sell? The seller was pushing this headache aside, but because Jamari followed up each week, when she was ready to make a deal (two weeks before foreclosure), Jamari was there to scoop it up and pass it to my team.

We've got $61,000 paid out, but this is only part of the seven-step entry fee to get in on this deal.

1. Seller's cash. In this case, that was $10,000.

2. Arrears. Here it was $41,000 to catch up payments.

3. Assignment fee. I paid Jamari $10,000 as an assignment fee.

4. Closing costs. These were around $5,000.

5. **Renovation.** I put about $20,000 into this renovation.
6. **Payments.** If you are doing repairs, you have to make payments on the property during these repairs. It could take ninety days. It could take six months. Factor these payments in. Mine were about $6,000 for this vacancy.
7. **Furniture.** This comes in when you're creating an Airbnb. I've heard some people use the $10-per-square-foot formula for Airbnb costs, but feel free to adjust based on your area and what you're trying to accomplish. I put in about $10,000 in furniture.

My initial investment is pretty heavy on this property, right? With our seven-step formula, we're in $102,000 right out of the gate. This scares a lot of people and that's understandable. It would have scared me in the beginning as well. But we've got the seller under contract and we have already spoken to the bank about a loan modification, so we know the deal is promising. After this refinancing, the deal dropped down to about $80,000 to start. This is still a huge number, so let's continue to see how this all played out. On this deal, I asked a lender to bring me $81,000, which includes a 10 percent interest charge. This number came to $8,100 per year for ten years, or $675 per month. For $675 per month, a private money lender covers all of the costs listed above.

That said, there are other things to consider. I've got to cover the principal, the interest, the taxes, and the insurance (PITI). This property also had an HOA. And, I also have to pay someone a management fee, because I don't want to manage the property myself. I'm in Phoenix, not Atlanta. And I don't even have an Airbnb account because I don't want to be involved with all of this. I work with a partner who manages all of my Airbnb deals. We've got:
1. PITI and HOA ($2,500)
2. Lender payment ($675)
3. Management fee ($1,000)
4. Miscellaneous budget for broken items ($700)
5. Utilities ($1,000)

My total cost per month to maintain this is $5,875. This is a higher-end deal, so the numbers are higher and the risk is higher. But here's the situation: On Airbnb, this property in Atlanta will bring in $11,000 per month on average, which means after all of my costs I'll net about $5,125 from a deal I didn't have to qualify for or cold-call for or talk to a bank about buying with a new mortgage. That's the beauty of good underwriting. I can buy a $700,000 house in Georgia with five bedrooms and five baths that will net me $5,125 per month.

STEP-BY-STEP UNDERWRITING

Examples aside, I want to get to the basics of underwriting. First of all, you need to gather all of your information. You are not able to underwrite a deal unless you have all of the information to do so. You need to know what the seller is asking for. You need to know what you want or what the buyer is looking for if you're doing a wholesale deal. Then it all comes down to acquisition strategies in terms of cash, subject-to, seller finance, or some sort of hybrid model. For me, again, the goal is to cash flow, which means it could be a rental, lease option, or wrap. But, if the property doesn't cash flow, you can also use a homestead buyer assignment, a wrap, or even a lease option.

Step 1. Gather up all the information you need to see if you can make the deal work. This includes:

- The ARV.
- The mortgage balance.
- The PITI.
- The rent rate.
- Whether or not there is cash flow.
- Finally, ask yourself if the entry fee is a deal killer or not.

You might find someone who is willing to do seller financing, but they want an outrageous down payment. You need to find out if the issue is just trust or if it is truly a financial concern. Let's say you find a $200,000 house that needs $50,000 in repairs and upgrades to become an Airbnb, but then the seller wants another $50,000 up front. This doesn't break the deal, but it's worse than a bank loan.

You just have to run your numbers and see if this makes sense after you consider all of the points in Step 1 and figure out what the loan payment will be. Then it depends on whether you can raise private money to make it work.

Step 2. Let's go a little deeper into the entry fee. As mentioned in the example above, the entry fee is made up of seven parts (cash to the seller, the arrears/late payment/liens, the cost of the acquisition, the closing costs, the renovation costs, the maintenance numbers, and the marketing costs). After you analyze this data, see if there is any wiggle room. You can figure out if there's more room in the deal than you originally thought (but don't make up numbers to imagine a deal works when it doesn't work). There are various exit strategies in terms of rent, lease option, wrap, and whether you can find private money. All of these options will change your data.

Step 3. Finally, you must consider your exit strategy. Can you wholesale the deal? Is it better as a buy and hold? Should you look for a homestead buyer (meaning a non-investor who wants to live in the house)? Each provides a different option, but there's a bit of a catch-22 to all of this. Yes, you can pay more in a seller finance deal, but if you overpay, you can no longer consider wholesaling as an option. Run all of the numbers to determine your exit strategy or potential exit strategies. Other options include:

- Wraps
- Lease options
- Sub-tail (sub-to, then sell retail)
- SRRR (seller finance, renovate, refinance, repeat)
- Vacation rentals (Airbnb, Vrbo, etc.)
- Group homes
- Corporate rentals

If you get really niche in your business, you will know immediately if the deal works within your exit strategy; then it's just a numbers game to find deals that fit your exit criteria.

There are countless ways to underwrite a deal, but the main goal is always to solve for X in a manner that makes you money. If there's a spread, there's a deal. It's not much more complicated than that. I paid over $40,000 to learn about subject-to and we've covered all of the basics in this short chapter. The more you know, the more options you have. As long as you understand these principles, you can start to close deals. As you scale, your numbers will grow because you also have to factor in your acquisition team. You make a little less per deal, but overall, like a franchise, you make more money as your business grows.

Profitability is all about PITI, cost of capital, HOA, and rental income. I want to walk through one more plug-and-play deal so you can see how all of this works. Let's use an example of a property I bought in Phoenix, Arizona. The current value of the home was $210,000 (the seller got this number from Zillow) with a purchase price of $180,000 (we negotiated this number based on the seller's $170,000 loan and the repairs needed on the home). The loan was for thirty years. The interest rate on the loan was 3 percent and the PITI was $843. For this deal, there wasn't an HOA to consider and the rent roll was $1,350 per month. Consider your information gathered.

What's next? This cold call lead accepted my offer because of her situation, which I'll cover in greater detail in the next chapter. June, the seller, had recently bought the house, but then her job required her to move to another state. She didn't want to get a renter or find someone to manage the property. She knew if she sold the house on the market, she would have had to cut a check and lose money on the deal because she didn't have any equity in the property. That was her motivation. That's why she sold to me subject-to. I explained sub-to to her so we could move the conversation from wholesale. I told her I could take over the mortgage payment and provide some cash for her. We settled on $10,000 in cash and I took over the existing mortgage of $170,000. She originally wanted $20,000 in cash, but I told her that I was not the buyer for her unless we could settle on $10,000. Eventually, she agreed to this amount.

Once I knew that my cash flow was $507 on this deal, I could figure out my total entry fee.

1. We paid June $10,000.

2. There were no arrears to consider.

3. The cost of the acquisition was $2,500. (My contract cost KPIs are $1,200 to pay for leads and employees. I base this number on total acquisition costs divided by deals received per month. The other $1,300 goes to the acquisition manager who locked in the deal.)
4. The closing costs were $2,500.
5. The renovation was about $2,000 because we had to do some minor repairs.
6. The maintenance was about $2,500 because I had to cover the mortgage during the repair and time to find a buyer.
7. Additionally, the marketing costs were $1,000.

The total entry fee was $20,500 to make the deal work. And, with this entry fee in mind, my initial cash flow of $507 was reduced to $371 because I had to pay back the private money covering this amount. My PITI was $843 minus the cost of capital—$136 from the rental income—which was $1,350.

In the end, the cash flow was $371, which is my income month after month while renters pay off the mortgage and everything else. For this deal, I used a free program called Rentometer, but you can also use tools like PropStream or the MLS. However, some of these programs have killed deals for us because the average numbers were lower than we would have brought in each month. Being able to spot some of this comes from experience, but just like in Step 1, you need to gather all of your information; more often than not, when you use free programs, they're not the most accurate for doing so.

In the next chapter, I'll be going over proven ways to address seller objections to create win/win scenarios. If you want to absorb more content before diving in, you can visit www.biggerpockets.com/creativewealth for videos, podcast episodes, and more on creative finance inspiration.

CHAPTER 9

Proven Scripts for Presenting the Offer

"Fear is weakness, learn from what experience teaches."

—NAS, "SELF CONSCIENCE"

When you first hear the phrase "subject-to," it can be a little daunting. Why would anyone break the mold and sell to you in a nontraditional manner? In reality, creative finance is better than the traditional model, as long as the seller understands how it works. It's your job to educate the seller, answer their questions, and make sure they understand everything they're potentially giving up with the traditional model. With the traditional retail model, yes, they can get a cash offer and they can get their listing price, but this comes with a number of cons.

Retail sales mean:

- Commission fees.
- Lowball offers.
- Capital gains tax.
- Delays.

- Rehabs before listings.
- Buyer loan approvals.
- Concessions.
- Repairs.

Not to mention issues where there's low equity in the house or something like a foreclosure or short sale, which will hit the seller's credit for a period of seven years. Knowing all these cons will help you eventually develop your own subject-to script, but for now, I want to break down individual objections and how to handle them. Here are some of the top questions you'll get as you try to explain creative finance, but specifically subject-to and seller financing.

"How did you get my information?"

If you're using some of the methods mentioned in this book, you may have gotten their information from either door knocking or using county records. Explain that you are a business and explain how you got their information in an honest way. If they're in foreclosure, they know it. If they own the property, it's public record. You're not on the phone or in person to sell them anything. You're there to give them money or help them make money. It's a service, not a solicitation. Treat it as such.

"I don't want terms. I want cash in hand…"

I generally ignore this initial comment, because it's the first objection you hear every single time. In Chapter 5, I pointed out that I didn't even respond when Marvin asked this. I continued to explain the situation to him to make sure he knew exactly what I meant by terms and why I can pay more with terms. After you've explained creative finance, if they still just want cash in hand, you have to find out why. Then you can figure out if a cash offer will work. But you need to know why they need money first and foremost. Then explain capital gains tax and walkaway money (money after commissions and everything else that comes with traditional retail), and make sure you're on the same page with the potential offer. Wholesale offers are always lower, so if they take a wholesale deal, it's often because they really need the money.

"Why don't you just buy the house the normal way?"

The seller wants you to buy in the traditional manner, because that's what they're used to and they like the idea of having a loaded bank account. But once you explain subject-to or creative finance, you can offer more than the other buyers who use this route. You also need to explain that you're running a business and you can only buy so many houses the traditional way. This is part of the bigger explanation of what it means to use creative finance.

"I want a large down payment."

"Want" and "need" are two different things. Most buyers will take anywhere from 0–5 percent down and we can generally put the down payment into the purchase price on the back end. This might include making payments at six-month increments, but it's creative, so do what works for you and the seller. Give them a few options if you need to as you gather more information. Whether or not they know it, they have a reason for every objection. Try to get to the heart of this objection in order to alter it. From your perspective, explain that you need to put the bulk of your money into rehab costs, closing costs, holding costs, and any other variables to make the deal work for you. Most importantly, though, if you can't make it work with your numbers, be willing to walk away. Don't just do deals to do deals. Build your custom portfolio.

"What is the interest rate?"

As you move through the conversation, they're going to ask about interest rates, especially if they're open to seller financing. I generally explain that that is something the "bank" would come up with, meaning I would like for them to make me an offer. I might give an example or talk about the national average, but I want the seller to come up with their own number first so I can negotiate with them. If we're doing a subject-to deal, I just take over whatever is currently in place until the loan is paid off in full. If we're doing seller finance on a deal where they own the property outright, I'm open to different rates as long as the numbers work in the end.

Time and Aliens

As you move further along into the conversation, the questions naturally get a little more complex. They're going to revolve around time and, sometimes, alien abductions . . . .

"I don't want to be tied up for thirty years..."

There are a handful of options to resolve this objection based on your circumstances. You can amortize the payment for thirty years (amortize refers to the amount of principal and interest paid each month over the course of the loan) and then do balloon payments of twenty years or fifteen years or ten years (balloon payments refer to a repayment on an outstanding principal sum at the end of a loan, which you can raise additional money for or refinance the original loan to pay off or just sell the property). If the seller is older, find out if you need to set up a trust or anything else for the seller's children to inherit payments after death. Like any situation, figure out what their problems are in order to solve their problems. Just because they don't want to do a long-term deal doesn't mean you can't find common ground or figure out something that works for both of you. Get creative. That's the whole game.

"What if I die or get abducted by aliens?"

As mentioned in the response to the last objection, payments can be passed along to a family member in the case of a death. As for me, the buyer, not making a payment (which has never happened and I make sure they know this), I explain about certain contingencies. First, we work with a title company, so they'll be alerted if a payment is ever missed. I also set up a performance deed, so they automatically get the property back within twenty-four hours of a missed payment. From their point of view, particularly in a foreclosure, this would be the best thing to happen to them. With a performance deed, I would catch up any arrears and fix up the house, then if I missed a payment, they would get the house back in a better state than they sold it, and they could sell it or do whatever else they want to do with it. If I feel a conversation moving into this common question, I'll start the question for them by saying, "What happens if I die or I'm abducted by aliens? That's your next question, right?" It lightens the mood while providing information.

"What if I want to buy another house?"

This question is really about having more than one mortgage open at a time during subject-to or seller finance. There's something called a DTI (debt-to-income) or declaration form that informs the lender about the situation. Generally speaking, the seller gets 75 percent of the total mortgage removed after one year and 100 percent of the mortgage removed the following year. Essentially, it doesn't affect their next loan if they want to buy another house in a traditional manner. However, I also offer to help them buy a home with subject-to so they can avoid these complications to begin with. Take some time to solve their problems and then there's no reason why they wouldn't want to work with you.

"What if you don't pay the mortgage?"

Again, this is about the performance deed that's put in place. A third-party company alerts the seller of any missed payments and confirms all made payments. If there's a missed payment, this document explains that the servicing company should automatically deed the house back to the seller. This takes away the seller's fear of having to take anyone to court. It's built with their safety and peace of mind right there in the contract.

"How do we handle the paperwork?"

It's done through a title company and an escrow officer. Some states use a lawyer rather than a title company, but the idea is to set up everything legally like a traditional sale. This protects both parties and makes sure everything is explained on paper in specific detail. I go into a little more detail in Chapter 14, but essentially you always want to have up-to-date paperwork and work with title agents or attorneys who understand creative finance and your business model. All paperwork should protect you and the seller.

"What if I get the house back damaged?"

This is a follow-up question to the performance deed one. My team has a strict underwriting process for tenants, so we don't rent to just anyone. We ensure quality tenants who have homeowner mindsets. We also have insurance in place to take care of specific damages. Plus, we have reserves in place, so our business is not going to miss a payment. There's never been a case where we gave the house back at all, much less damaged. As you figure out your own model, be honest and create your own plan for this question based on what your business is capable of doing.

"What if the house burns down?"

For this, it would all go through the insurance company. The mortgage would get paid off in full and the seller would get back the difference. This is another win-win situation for the seller, which is what we're trying to convey with the negotiation. I haven't personally experienced this, but it's certainly a possibility. It is imperative that you make sure that your insurance is up to date, and don't ever let a lapse put you or the seller at risk, particularly in a subject-to deal.

Exit Strategy Questions

For various reasons, sellers want to know what you plan to do with the house. These questions could be personal or business related, or they could just be questions of curiosity.

"What will you do with the house?"

In my business we have eight exit strategies. In any given call, I explain the one that makes the most sense to the seller, but I may also list some other options if we're truly not sure what we're going to do with the house. Our strategies include:

- Wholesale.
- Wraps.
- Lease options.
- SRRR.
- Sub-tail.
- Vacation rentals.
- Group homes or assisted living.
- Corporate rentals.

Explain the ones that make the most sense for you and for the deal. If the seller has a personal connection to the house, I'm careful with the phrasing I use as I give an explanation. Be empathetic, especially if they're sentimentally attached to the property. For you it's a piece of the overall portfolio, but they could have real emotions wrapped up in the deal.

"Are you going to rent out the house?"

This could just be a question of curiosity, but always explain your exit strategy so they understand your business model and know you can make the payments. If you're dealing with a tired landlord, they may just be curious why you want to take over a place where the renters have created negative experiences in the past. Explain your business model in a concise manner so they understand. You can also explain your underwriting process so they know you have money in reserves for any issues. We're trying to create a hassle-free deal, not something that will come back to bite them in six months when they never wanted the headache in the first place.

"How will I get paid?"

We use a servicing company to ensure all parties and accounts are paid on time. You can repeat the idea of the performance deed so they understand what happens if a payment is ever missed. I don't miss payments, and it's not good business to miss payments. The same answer is true for "How will the mortgage get paid?" Be honest and figure out a reliable payment method based on the deal.

"I want the money up front to reinvest."

This is an interesting comment that I get quite often. They want the money to invest in something else, but they rarely know what "something else" they want to invest in, so why not invest in real estate? Stocks are generally speculation and most people get less than 8 percent return, so I try to make a deal that beats this return. In real estate, aka the oldest investment strategy in America, you're investing in something tangible. Explain how they can make more money as a lender than an investor. If you do the deal right, they might be open to working with you as a private money investor on future deals.

"I need money to move…"

This is another question that is really about the down payment. Figure out what they need to move and try to make it work. You may have to take out a personal loan or work with private money for a larger down payment, but the more problems you can solve, the better deal you can make. You can also provide things like a moving truck or temporary storage if it feels necessary to close the deal. Get creative and provide value. Make the deal work.

"When will you take over payments?"

For subject-to deals, this is all about when the seller vacates the property. I try to close within thirty to sixty days, but it all depends on that particular situation. The real answer to this question is whenever you can completely take over the property from the seller. From your point of view, you have to factor in making payments on the mortgage while you're doing any repairs or looking for a renter. If you're doing a fix-and-flip, it's likely going to take you a few months. If you're brand-new, get the contractor timelines up front and expect obstacles and roadblocks, because they're inevitable.

"How do I get equity?"

As long as I can get the terms I need, I'm open to the seller refinancing the property to take money out of the deal. A lot of things have to work out for this to happen, but it's certainly possible. That said, with the SRRR and BRRRR methods, I can do the same thing. I can refinance over time to make some extra money on the property.

Negotiations for a Better Deal

As the seller understands more and more about your business, they may start to realize you can beat all other offers. This is the real negotiation phase.

"I want a better deal..."

A lot of sellers want to have their cake and eat it too, but it's your job to find out what they mean by "a better deal." As we went over in previous chapters, you have to make sure they understand their true walkaway money. After traditional deals scoop all of the profits off the top, the seller is generally making less than they think. But, if they're open to seller financing or subject-to, I'm open to paying more. It's all about the terms for me. I will tell the seller, "You get the price you want and I get the terms I need."

"When do I need to leave?"

I usually have my cold caller ask their time frame up front, because my time frame is based on their situation. We want to move quickly, but this isn't always possible. I work with their time frame and make plans to take over payments as soon as they vacate the property. If you have other variables in place, make sure to factor those in as well, like scheduling repairs or buying furniture for an Airbnb or whatever your model might be.

"I can't do terms, because I want to buy another house."

This is a similar question to others we've already covered, but I'll answer it again here. We use a form called a DTI (debt-to-income) declaration form that helps lenders understand this scenario. It explains that someone else is making payments in their name on the initial mortgage. The seller gets 75 percent of the total mortgage removed after one year and 100 percent of the mortgage removed the following year. Essentially, it doesn't affect their next loan if they want to buy another house in a traditional manner. However, I also offer to help them buy a home with subject-to so they can avoid all of these complications to begin with.

"I'm in foreclosure or a short sale..."

Many times, we can pay for the arrears and catch up the foreclosed seller to "current," which means they will no longer be in pre-foreclosure. This means that their credit will not be affected negatively to that point as long as we hold the account, because we have reserves and systems in place to not miss payments. Also, over time, we will help improve their credit score due to the mortgage payment consistency and the fact that there are no longer any missed or late payments. Plus, if there is an issue, we have documents in place that deed the house back to the original owner.

"Will this affect my credit score?"

If the seller is in arrears or pre-foreclosure, the deal will affect their credit score, but in a positive way. There's no actual charge to the credit when we take over payments, but we're making payments in their name, so their credit will improve over time.

"Will my heirs receive anything if I die?"

We can set up any number of scenarios in the contract that say anyone they choose can be the successor of payments if anything should happen to the original seller. This is particularly important if the seller is older and thinking about leaving money to heirs. However, if they don't have a successor, we can also set up terms so they receive money in balloon payments after a period of time or even donate it to charity. This guarantees that an older person with no heir in place gets their money in a timely manner.

Key Categories to Close

Now that we've covered most of the common objections, let's talk about some big-picture ideas for your sub-to script. You want to think about five key categories, which are:

1. Strength of introduction.
2. Rapport building.
3. Fact-finding/motivation.
4. Overcoming objections.
5. Presentation of solutions.

When I start my introduction with a new seller, I try to get straight to the point and let them know why I'm calling them in the first place. Hopefully, if you're using my cold-calling strategies, you've already had a VA set up the initial appointment, and now it's just time to close. But if you're wearing every hat in your business, one way to start would be to simply say:

"Hey, this is [your name] and I'm calling from [company name]. I'm looking to buy some properties in your area. Are you still the owner of [address]?"

After the seller confirms, you can add:

"Great, let me set the stage a little for you. I'm calling because my company is looking to buy four to five properties in your area. If you're open to selling, this will only take a few minutes of your time."

Next, you want to start to build rapport. If you're a local investor, this would be a good time to quickly tell your story. One of my students uses this example when talking to tired landlords:

"Great, I appreciate your time today. My wife and I are just getting started in this area and looking to buy our

first investment properties. What has been your experience with renters in the area?"

This way, you get the seller to talk about themselves as they answer your questions. If the seller is a tired landlord, you can connect over having bad tenants if that's something you've also experienced. If the seller is preparing to move, connect about their relocation. If the seller is going through a family struggle, take their side of the struggle and continue to build rapport.

As you start to connect with the seller, continue to do additional fact-finding. In many cases, you'll uncover more and more the longer you talk. What's the real reason they want to sell? What is their true motivation? A lot of sellers will say they don't plan to sell, but then talk to you for thirty minutes on the phone. Everyone says they're willing to sell if the price is right, but it's your job to find out if they're serious about this, and then figure out what that number is. Their motivation could be negative cash flow or costly repairs or foreclosure or anything in between. Get to the root of their problem so you can be the solution.

Then it's time to overcome objections. For sellers, it can be complicated to sell a house. They're on their own fact-finding mission; you're going to have to jump through some hoops to acquire the deal. Some of this is about providing information, while other parts are about negotiation. Refer back to this chapter so you know all of the typical questions, but understand that sellers are complex and they could ask questions not listed here.

Finally, offer your solution. Tell them about subject-to or seller finance or cash or whatever your game plan is to help them with their problem. If they need help moving, offer a solution. If they need help clearing out the house, offer a solution. If they need help moving out a late tenant, offer a solution. You need to be the one-stop-shop problem solver, because if you're not, they're just as likely to go with someone else. If you can build rapport and provide a real solution, the seller will choose you to buy their home. Remember my anecdote about how I once offered to relocate some bunny rabbits? Because of this unique offer, they remembered me when it was time to sell.

INVESTOR STORY
Mitch Roye—Joint Venture Deal
"There's always a solution to the problem."

Mitch Roye said self-defeating negative self-talk kept him from closing his first deal for years. Now he's a leader in the sub-to community. For this deal, Mitch partnered with another investor named Richard Knowles. Together, thanks to an optimistic approach, they were able to close a major deal.

This deal took about six months to close. The seller had five properties in California to sell, including an out-of-service gas station with an attached residential structure. They were all on the same piece of land, some literally connected to the others. There was also a triplex and two duplexes in the bunch. They were all in pretty bad condition. The seller's motivation was that the properties were run-down and vacant.

Mitch and Richard started with a cash offer, but the seller wouldn't budge. After going back and forth a while, they eventually presented an option contract, which means they'd have the option to sell it, but the seller could also sell it to someone else. This gave them the option to sell it for the seller, which means they would make money on the deal but they could also walk away from the deal. For these, it's always a good idea to be honest with your plans and tell the seller you're not 100 percent sure you can sell it with an assignment. Be transparent as you hunt down a buyer.

Mitch and Richard eventually ended up renewing the thirty-day option contract five or six times. They were able to do this because they were transparent and they were showing up as problem solvers, not just investors. Over the next few months, they kept looking for buyers, then decided to do a flat-fee MLS listing. This led to a few tire-kickers, but then a developer reached out.

This was the most complex deal Richard and Mitch had ever done, and included the seller chasing off a Realtor with a machete. But as they faced each minor roadblock, they continued to bring people together, present options, and move forward inch by inch. When they got the offer from the developer, the seller agreed to carry some of the debt, so they moved into a Morby Method deal, where the seller carries twenty percent of the transaction.

In escrow, the problems started again. The lender wouldn't fund the commercial property, so they removed the gas station from the initial transaction, meaning they had to move it to a separate commercial transaction. This meant they had to structure it as a seller-carryback on the gas station, while the buyer would fund the four residential properties. At this point, most people would give up, but not Mitch and Richard.

Now they had two escrow agreements, one residential and one commercial. Then escrow told the title company that the commercial and residential parts of the gas station were attached, so title wouldn't insure the deal. They had to take the attached residential and move it to the commercial transaction. They thought they had solved this problem, but when they moved the fourth residential property to commercial, they lowered the overall value of the other three residential properties, causing another issue.

The buyer's lender would no longer fund the full amount, so negotiations essentially had to start over. In the end, the duo lowered their rate to make it work. They came up with two options. They could either have the seller carry a second position or they could find another escrow and title company. They didn't like the second option, so the seller agreed to carry a larger debt load on the commercial deal and a new debt load on the residential deal.

All of this was done to lower risk for all parties. They basically had to create two separate Morby Methods. The final number for the residential transaction was $600,000. A lender gave the buyer $525,000 and the final $75,000 was carried seller finance. With a large enough down payment on the purchase price, the seller was happy enough to then offer seller financing, which is the Morby Method. The commercial transaction was $950,000 with a full seller carry. Since the buyer had already spent $525,000, Richard and Mitch suggested the seller offer the $75,000 from the residential deal back to the buyer to help renovate the properties. The total price was $1,550,000 for the full deal. It only worked out because Mitch and Richard were open to trying new strategies and open to coming up with lots and lots of options.

Most of the challenges you run into start after you open escrow and get your contract. Most people think everything happens before escrow. In this scenario, most people would have walked away from this deal. But after everything was said and done, Mitch and Richard made $80,000 on the deal, which they split with the agent. What's most interesting is that they also learned essentially $5 million of mastery in terms of escrow and more. Plus, the new person who JV'd on the deal (joint ventured between two parties) also got paid and this was their first deal.

KEY TAKEAWAY | If you never give up and you always look for a solution to seemingly unsolvable problems, you'll be the last one standing when it's time to cash in on the deal.

CHAPTER 10

Things to Do Before You Start

"I'm just tryna carry out my own legacy / but the place I call home ain't letting me."

—**JOEY BADA$$, "LIKE ME"**

Legacy. That's the best way to describe your business. When you think about your business in terms of it being a legacy, that removes any small pressure for overnight success or any ideas of a get-rich-quick scheme. It's a legacy. It's the underlying bedrock for generational wealth. Yes, you can make money right away, but you always need to think about the future. It's not just laying bricks; it's building a cathedral. Every small action is for a larger purpose. It's through the micro that we can build the macro.

When you're starting out as a real estate investor, you may have a dream to acquire a hundred doors or complete financial freedom or something along those lines, but it's almost impossible to achieve financial freedom if you start with a shaky foundation. When it's time to create your company, you need to know how to move in the right direction along a proven path. I've worked with a lot of great minds to build my own structure, but as you read this chapter, understand that this isn't hard-and-fast advice, but a path that worked for me. You need to figure out which of these methods works for you based on your buy box, your business model, and your big-picture goals.

First, let's talk about company structures. The majority of entity options fall into categories like sole proprietorship, general partnership, limited liability company (LLC), limited liability partnership, S corp, and C corp. When we did our Zero to Hero Challenge, we encouraged the initial hundred participants to use an LLC. I would not recommend going out and making deals without the umbrella protection of having an LLC in place. It's not safe for you. It's not safe for the seller. We live in a sue-first economy. An LLC protects your assets and your family from these types of mistakes. Likewise, not having a company set up makes you liable for paying tens of thousands of dollars in taxes, which could be a write-off for your business. S corp and C corp are how you file your taxes, so you can have an LLC and file as an S corp, but this isn't legal or accounting advice, so speak with professionals in your area who work with real estate investors and understand what you're trying to accomplish. Personally, I work with a company called Prime Corporate Services (PCS) and I have several LLCs in place depending on different types of deals and different partnerships. I have LLCs that do business with other LLCs that I own, all through PCS. Recently, I've also partnered with PCS for our Gator Method events and some of our other challenges, because everyone needs an LLC in their real estate business.

A sole proprietorship is an unincorporated business with a single owner who pays taxes as an individual. A lot of real estate agents or loan officers have sole proprietorships. Some pros to this option are that it's free to set up, there's not much paperwork, you can deduct business losses against personal income, and it's just one extra form to fill out when tax time comes around. But there are also cons, like the fact that you have no liability protection, it's harder to get a business loan, it's tough to build business credit, and you have to pay taxes at a personal income rate. I've never gotten a business loan as a sole proprietor, so I recommend the LLC route. However, you can start as a sole proprietor and then get an LLC later on.

With a general partnership you have an arrangement where two or more owners manage and operate the business and share in both profits and losses. This might be for a tradesperson, a small business, or just a new business with lower liability potential. I like to think of this as the dating phase. You might set this up with a partner in the early stages before you eventually decide the business is worthy of an LLC. Like a sole proprietorship, setup is easy, there are no paperwork requirements, there are no annual meetings, and you can deduct business expenses or losses against personal income. That said, each owner is personally responsible for the debts of the company, it's tough to get a business credit or loan, and the company can easily unravel if the relationship goes sour (also like dating).

A limited liability partnership is a general partnership that offers protection against liability at a degree varying from state to state. This applies to jobs with licenses or degrees like doctors, attorneys, accountants, and licensed financial advisors. This type of partnership is based on the state you live in, not super expensive to set up, and doesn't have to have additional rules for reporting like corporations do. Partners can leave without having to dissolve the company, and it's good for investors who don't want to take on a liability. But general partners still have personal liability and limited partners can end up with liability if they take on too active a role in the company. I would recommend doing some outside research beyond this book and speaking with professionals to determine what is best for you.

An LLC is a corporate structure whereby the members of the company are not personally responsible for the company's debts or liabilities. LLC is a hybrid model that combines characteristics of a corporation and a partnership or sole proprietorship. It works well for real estate investors and many small businesses. I look at an LLC as its own entity. A client can sue an LLC, but not the person behind the LLC. If I own a group of homes and one house gets a lawsuit, my insurance will likely take care of the lawsuit. However, if there's a one-in-a-million lawsuit where they wipe out the LLC's assets, there's no way for them to get to you personally as long as you follow the proper guidelines. It's also not that expensive to set up an LLC. It can be taxed as a partnership or corporation, and you don't have all the additional rules that corporations do. That said, it is a pass-through entity and the LLC can still be sued. I own twenty-five LLCs at the moment and I have a bookkeeper manage everything for us so we can just check the data for growth.

What's an S corp? This is how I file my taxes. An S corporation is best for midsize businesses. It's the light version of a C corp. It offers an investment opportunity and perpetual existence, and you can file taxes yearly to avoid double taxation. It's a major advantage for people running their own business who want to avoid insane personal taxes. You can also split up income between salary and dividends to save on social security. A C corp is for a larger company, like Coca-Cola or Facebook. I don't have a C corp, but I do know people who use C corps for fix-and-flip businesses, so this is up to you and your business. It's expensive to create and there's double taxation, but it's easier to raise money if you're doing serious business as an investor.

One reason I have so many LLCs is that there are ways to avoid the capital gains tax. If you flip houses as a business, there's no capital gains tax. If you flip houses to wholesale them, there is a capital gains tax. It depends if you're selling a product or you're a vendor. It can get a little complicated and there's no reason to obsess over these things up front, but you are building a legacy, so you should always be working to make the most of your business. Don't pay Uncle Sam excess money that should stay in your pocket.

The Financial War Chest

After you set up your business to be structurally sound, it's time to build your financial war chest. I like to set up a three-part system where I:

1. Pay myself.
2. Set aside money for future marketing.
3. Add some money to the war chest.

Let's break this down in a hypothetical deal. Say I buy a property for $100,000. Then I wrap it to a homestead buyer for $170,000. In that process, I collect 10 percent up front, so that's $17,000. Maybe it costs about $7,000 to get into the deal for paying the seller or some closing costs. Basically, I would get an up-front fee of $10,000 for making this deal. When you do a deal like this, you need to allocate the deal properly. In this $10,000 scenario, $3,000 goes to paying myself. That's my grocery money. That's my house payment. Next, I take out another $3,000 for future marketing and overhead. That includes paying any employees, paying my electric bill, and those types of things. Finally, with the last $4,000, I put this in my financial war chest. This money goes to emergencies, evictions, defaults, and everything else that might derail my business or anything that pops up out of my control.

For any property, your goal should be to set aside three months of mortgage payments and another $2,500 for any minor renovations. If the example above has a $1,000 mortgage to the seller, then you need to have $3,000 + $2,500 = $5,500 set aside. This is your war chest. Even if you do some minor renovations, you always want to have that additional $2,500 set aside in case your tenant leaves or anything else like that happens. Then you can repeat the process and do so without having to worry about pulling any money from your own pocket. You want to do this for every single deal.

For the entry fee in the example above, I'm a little short on my war chest. When this happens, what I like to do is build up the war chest over time. It doesn't get covered right away, but I've got cash flow set up. If the rent or mortgage that I'm paid is $1,600 and I only have to pay $1,000, I cash flow $600 per month. That means when I bring in that $600 cash flow, I can put away $200 per month and slowly build up my war chest. It's not a perfect system, because there is some lag time in the beginning, but we're thinking long-term. We always want to make sure we have the security of the financial war chest in place. If you're in larger markets or doing more expensive deals, obviously you'll want to have a larger war chest. It's a ratio, not a one-size-fits-all number. If you find you need additional expenses, make adjustments accordingly. If you're in the beginning of your investment career, don't fall into the trap of going out to buy a new car or a Rolex. Build your financial war chest, utilize a plan of attack, set some aside to pay yourself, and be smart with your money.

CHAPTER 11

Finding Buyers for My Deals

"The grass ain't always green, the meat ain't always lean."

—GHOSTFACE KILLAH, "NUGGETS OF WISDOM"

How do you find a buyer for a creative finance deal? In my particular scenario, since I'm married to a Unicorn Realtor, I generally have my wife, Laura, list the property on the MLS. However, in my experience, the majority of real estate agents "keep the blinders on" and only focus on traditional real estate sales. In the past, I've wasted a ton of hours explaining what seller financing is or what subject-to is or any number of other creative finance strategies. We just post on the MLS as a backup. In addition to the MLS, we post on Facebook Marketplace and Craigslist. When I post on Craigslist, I put a rental ad out instead of a for-sale ad.

In this case, I'm looking for people who think they can only rent. Since I'm the bank in these scenarios, they don't need perfect credit. I get way more applications with a rental ad, but in the post, I include a rent-to-own program as another option. I set up a phone system that tells them to press 1 to rent and press 2 to "buy with bad credit but you have a down payment," and then I only talk to those people who press 2. I don't even listen to those who just press 1. My team currently uses a program called CallRail for this filtering system and we use the same program for our bandit sign phone number.

Something unique I do is go to lenders and mortgage officers who have a ton of clients. They help me sell a lot of properties, because they're tuned in to the right networks of people. I give them a kickback, where we might pay for their marketing, so they don't break any rules or laws. A lot of mortgage loans are turned down, so they send them to credit repair. More often than not, that client doesn't come back. But they've got lists of people who have been recently turned down. The officer tells them, "If you're looking for a home, here's a guy who does seller finance," and then that person contacts me. If I can make it work, my team will try to help them.

More often than not, these are the most qualified buyers. They're not qualified in the traditional manner, but they're super qualified for my types of deals. I don't care if they had a foreclosure years earlier or if they get paid under the table for work if they've got the down payment and steady income. It takes time to build a relationship with a mortgage officer, but it's highly profitable, especially when you do multiple deals like this every month. The same is true for connecting with credit repair companies. Their clients are generally fixing their credit to buy a house, so if I approach the company and say I can help their clients buy a house before they even finish the process. I pay them a $1,000 kickback fee. I get around 30 percent of my buyers from credit repair companies like this and it works out for everybody.

Specific Techniques

You don't want to lock up contracts and then have to cancel because you can't find a buyer. Currently, my team uses a dozen methods to find buyers; some are simple (Craigslist) and others are more complex (SEO, or search engine optimization). All of these strategies work, and we use a variety of methods because we sell in a multitude of ways.

On Craigslist, the first thing you should do is research how people are listing ads in that given area. For whatever reason, there are different terminologies and techniques in different areas across the United States. One location might say something in a different way or just highlight different terms. Look around to see what works and adapt to that particular market. Go into your market's Craigslist and type in "rent to own" or "seller finance" or "lease option" or "no bank needed" and see what types of ads pop up. This will give you an indication of how strong the seller finance model is in any particular area. I've never seen an area with zero competitors. People have been doing this for years, so look for models that work in your location.

In addition to gathering information, this method will introduce you to other creative investors in your market. I like to reach out and say something simple like:

"Hey [name], I see that you're a creative investor. I also do creative investing. Maybe we can trade deals? Maybe we can trade buyers if I have the buyers that need something you've got? Then if you have a buyer that needs something, we can swap."

Say whatever you like, but introduce yourself to as many local creative investors as you can find to do deals together. Some of my best friends have come from just reaching out on Craigslist in this manner.

Next, we post on Facebook Marketplace. There's been a big push toward Facebook Marketplace over the past few years. It's somewhat phasing out Craigslist, but not entirely, and which is more successful depends on the area. I would recommend doing both unless you do a few tests and find a clear frontrunner. Likewise, you can use this method to find other creative investors and you can even create a dummy ad to see if investors or buyers are engaging with your ads. See what works and what doesn't work. If you do post a dummy ad, you can say you already sold the house from the ad, but ask what they're looking for and what kind of down payment they have. Then you can cater to these people with your next deal.

Then there are credit repair companies. This has moved up on our list of successful strategies. To find local companies, just Google phrases like "credit repair companies in [your area, state, city, or town]." The script I use for this technique is essentially this:

"Hi [name], I do a lot of seller financing and I want to add value to your business and to your clientele, whom I know are currently trying to rebuild their credit so they can go out and buy a house. I offer 'no bank involved' seller financing and lease options. I would like to know if you would like to bring your buyers to the table and I could give you a referral fee. A lot of our credit repair companies charge us $500 to $1,000, where a Realtor would charge 3 percent or more."

This gets the ball rolling and can be a solid referral system for your business.

Collaboration over Competition

If you've been following me on social media, you see that I hang out with my competition every single day. Not only are we friends, but sometimes we even go out and create businesses together. We may compete in one area and collaborate in another. That's why we have so many successful businesses, from mobile home developments to digital notaries. You need to collaborate more than you compete. Currently, I have over sixteen streams of income and I collaborate on every single business that I own.

I realized that collaborating with people who have skills and talents that I don't have will make me more successful. I might compete with a competitor on a wholesaling deal and then partner with that same wholesaler in another area of the business. Because of these strong relationships, where we're all open to share notes and talk about tactics, we can all grow in a multitude of ways. Over time we build trust and that is key to our success.

In addition, since so many people look at everyone else as competition, I'm confident that I can approach someone to collaborate with simply because I'm open to collaboration. The same is true for finding buyers. I give away as much information as possible online, and often I end up partnering with followers to do deals. Call it karma or whatever, but this service-first mindset has been the secret of my fast growth and the growth of many of my students.

When I meet someone new, I like to ask, "What are you struggling with and how can I help?" Sometimes I even say, "How are you paying your bills today?" This is a way to exchange value with people and make real connections. I want to tell people about my business and hear things about their business, so we can all move forward together.

When it comes to finding cash buyers, this might be asking about their buy box. I hosted a training with Laura called "How to Find a Deal in 2 Hours" in which we talked about Unicorn Realtors, but also how to find cash buyers. In that training, I taught followers how to use a system to filter out cash purchasers in the last twelve months in any given area who were also listed as an LLC rather than just as an individual homeowner. Then we skip-traced that list to find real cash buyers who own or flip properties in that area. After that, you simply need to call these cash buyers and ask them about their buy box. Find out what they're looking to buy. So many people try to get the deal before they have a buyer, but this is putting the cart before the horse. You need to know what you're looking for so when you do find a deal, you can make it work. Get your list of cash buyers and ask them their criteria.

- Do they care about occupancy status?
- Do they care about mailing vacancies?
- Does it have to be residential? If so, what size? What price point?
- Are they interested in all types of residential like mobile homes, duplexes, townhouses, etc.?

You can gather some of this information before the call as the properties they own should be listed online, but it's possible they have multiple LLCs or any number of other privacy filters in place. Either way, you can find anywhere from a few dozen to a few hundred cash buyers depending on the area. Make these calls. Build relationships. Figure out what they want before you approach them with something they don't want.

This is one way I explain what I can bring to the table in any given business. I was once on a podcast where I gave out my cell phone number to about 12,000 listeners. Several people contacted me, but only one approached me in a way that made sense for us to collaborate. That was Cody Barton, who's now my business partner. We now own a cold call center together. We own a few apps together. We own a wholesale business together. We do some fix-and-flips together. I wouldn't have built these businesses with anybody else.

Here's what Cody did differently than everyone else: Cody said, "If I can bring you leads, would you help me close them? You can take the majority of the profit, I'm just not good at closing leads." As a sales guy, I loved this idea. Cody started off bringing value to the table first. Within a few weeks, we had closed a few deals and found it made sense to go into a few other businesses together. I took Cody from not closing deals to closing hundreds of deals as a team. We will inevitably create a portfolio worth tens of millions over the next few decades. Most people would have looked at Cody as a competitor, but instead, we collaborated. We created an environment of expectations and clarity that we wanted to live in. We moved from competitors to friends to business partners. Likewise, you need to be making friends with everyone. Your competition is going to bring you resources. They're not competitors, they're collaborators. Use them. Serve them. Find ways to build up those around you and the results will come.

I'm part of a mastermind in Arizona with over thirty other wholesalers. If you think about how every member of that group is spending at least an hour a day reading, researching, and learning more about the business, when we all get together, we each have access to thirty-plus bonus hours of research per day. That's what is amazing about collaboration. We squash any negative feelings, show up to be as transparent as possible, and then the group itself becomes a shortcut to success for all participants. Together, we crowdsource industry information that only helps all of our businesses. The more tools in your tool belt, the better your business will be.

Negotiating Deals

Negotiating deals is one of my favorite things to do. It's why I record a lot of my calls. I like to think of it as game footage. How can I get better? Where did I make a mistake? What clue or small thing did I miss? Was there a better way to solve that problem? This is true for seller calls, but it's also true for finding buyers. It's all a negotiation. If I don't get the deal, I will go back and listen to the call. I analyze the call like a sports coach analyzes a game to see how their team can improve and build strategy for the next game. Maybe I missed something. Maybe I should have paused. Maybe I should have asked better questions. This isn't always the case when I close a deal, but I do like recording the calls to get better and to help me teach others how to negotiate deals. Negotiating is where the deal gets done. We can talk to motivated sellers all day, but if we don't know how to negotiate, we're never going to close deals and make the business work.

First things first: Buyers are liars and sellers are worse. If you've watched me online, you've heard me say this a few thousand times. It should be written on my tombstone, because it's the truth. And it's all part of the negotiation. The origin of this is based on the idea that a buyer will tell you anything to get a good deal. Yes, that happens. But sellers are the exact same way. If you're negotiating a deal where you're buying from a seller to sell to a buyer, you're getting hit by both sides with lies. Even little old ladies are going to lie to you. Actually, they're the best at it. They're professional liars because you feel like they're telling you the truth, but they're not. Think about it: It's a little old lady who has somehow acquired a few dozen homes in her portfolio. She's not foolish. She's a pro. That's how she got the portfolio in the first place. Both sellers and buyers are manipulating you along the way, so you need to knock down those barriers and figure out the truth in each situation to make the deal work.

My team recently had a seller whom our door knocker found. We found out the seller had two properties they were willing to sell. Then one of our cold callers reached out to the same seller; they're calling thousands of lists, so they didn't know our door knocker had already approached this seller. As we entered the negotiation phase, we found out the seller was playing us against ourselves. We had a door knocker and a cold caller, and she wanted to get the best deal for these two properties. Whenever she got information from one party, she would use it against the other party. We finally figured out we were negotiating the same deal in two different approaches and that this sweet little old lady who owned the house was a dynamic liar. She would tell one thing to the cold caller and something else to the door knocker. Our door knocker closed one deal, but she kept telling our cold caller that she still had both properties available. They're not big lies and it's to be expected, but you need to know what you're getting into when you start to negotiate. Sellers lie and misinform until they feel comfortable and start to trust you. They only tell you the truth when they feel comfortable with you. That's why you need to build rapport and create relationships with these people. We should have told her that she was speaking with two parts of one company, but we figured this out too late and were not able to do that in this situation.

How do you make a seller feel comfortable? You have to educate the seller. You have to present options. You have to ask explorative questions. I approach each situation as an educator. If they describe a situation to me and I'm not the right buyer for the deal, I will try my best to present them options and suggestions to help find the right buyer. You need to tell this to the seller as quickly as possible. I'm constantly telling sellers that I'm not the right buyer, but I'm open to presenting other ideas. I'm able to do this because I have a specific strategy in mind to fit my overall buy box. The more people I talk to and educate, the better I get at my job and my business.

Another exploratory question I start with is: "Get me up to speed. How are other real estate investors or Realtors treating you?" This is a good way to get the seller to open up and get the conversation going. Instead of saying, "What other offers are you getting?" which is hostile, you approach the question in a way that helps bring down the seller's natural barriers. You find out if they're meeting with other people and what kind of deals they might be open to versus those they don't want and why they haven't signed already. Ask, "Are you looking for something they haven't provided yet?" Let them tell you a story to figure out what kind of journey they've been on. I want to know where they are at in the process so I can figure out if I'm the solution to their problem or not. I might be the solution and I might not be, but I need all of the facts there to either close the deal or help them find a better solution. It's more difficult to solve a math equation if you're missing multiple variables, so always work to narrow down the problem to find the solution.

INVESTOR STORY
Munif Saza—Airbnb Arbitrage
"How Liquid Are You?"

Munif Saza originally started training as investor on the weekends. Now he's a well-known leader in the group who specializes in creative finance and Airbnb deals. At the time, he worked nine-to-five as an engineer and signed up to watch the 7:00 a.m. role-playing-style training—known as "The Daily Dial"—before his normal job. At the time, he wasn't a good closer and he's since become one of the best closers in the business. He's since quit his job and moved to Arizona to close more deals more often.

Munif's goal is to help other people close deals. He got started calling other people's sellers for free. He didn't care about the money and the people generating leads didn't have time to talk to sellers. They both felt like there was nothing to lose. Munif would make calls for about two hours per day, seven days a week. Then, once he got his footing, he started to split assignment fees with sellers, and that created his business.

The current home Munif lives in is an Airbnb arbitrage, which means it's a 100 percent financed space where a renter brings in additional income from subletting all or part of it. He found a landlord through a referral: A friend lived in the back unit and had moved out. Munif asked if he could take over that unit.

Munif offered to apply, but when he got to talking with the landlord, the landlord said, "I live in the main unit, but it's too big for me. I shouldn't have bought this place." Munif asked about the mortgage, which was $3,500 for both. Munif asked if he could rent both units for $3,800 so the landlord would cashflow $300 per month; then Munif could live in the small back unit and could Airbnb the main unit.

The main unit brings in $8,000 per month, which means Munif gets paid to live in Phoenix: He lives for free and makes an additional $4,200 per month for setting up the deal. And, after he got married, he switched to the big unit. Now he makes a little less but still profits from the overall Airbnb deal. But that's not even the main deal.

After months of working this deal, the same landlord asked if Munif wanted another Airbnb deal that was only a few miles away. It was even better than the original offer, so Munif agreed to do the deal. "But I think we need $30,000 to furnish the deal. How liquid are you?" he asked his new landlord. Munif offered 10 percent over the $30,000 for furnishing. He doesn't own either deal, but he cash flows from both opportunities and expects to make more than $8,000 from the second property since it's bigger and more desirable.

Why doesn't the owner just do this himself? It's not his business model and he's got too much going on to learn a new one. This particular guy hates management. He could even hire a management company and replicate the model, but he trusts Munif and understands the situation that will happen from working with Munif.

As the economy shifts over time, up and then down, there are going to be more and more deals like this, where a house has been freshly renovated but the seller can't make what they need to make. This is where you can come in with an Airbnb arbitrage deal. It's just like my mom getting supplies from Michaels and selling products. Everyone gets paid and everyone wins, but you can win the most if you can find more and more opportunities like this. However, there are also disadvantages—you're putting in a lot of work but you don't get appreciation or depreciation or the other benefits of owning the property. In Munif's case, he hopes to buy the property in the end, but that's currently up in the air as he's still in the deal. Arbitrage gets you in the game with cash flow, but there are pros and cons.

KEY TAKEAWAY | You don't even need to own the deal to make money on the deal. Look for creativity wherever you can find it, because it's everywhere. Just because one solution works for you doesn't mean it works for everyone else.

CHAPTER 12

Ways to Fund My Deals If I'm Broke

"Even though you're fed up, you got to keep ya head up."
—TUPAC, "KEEP YA HEAD UP"

If you're skipping ahead, this chapter is not about traditional financing. I don't care what it takes to secure a bank loan and neither should you. Not in the beginning. Not when you're trying to scale your real estate investment business. When we talk about funding, we're mainly talking about seller financing and raising private money. Where do you find private money lenders? Where do you find people who will invest in your real estate business? Which documents do you need? Let me explain using a case study situation where I helped a student raise $60,000 for a particular deal.

First, let's talk about the lender's point of view. Why would anyone want to give you $60,000 or more in the first place? Most banks give you less than 1 percent return for your savings account where a private lender gets anywhere from 8–15 percent return on their investment for a short-term loan. This means anyone with some extra money can potentially become a private money lender.

Doctors, lawyers, friends, family, janitors, nurses . . . anyone with a few grand to invest. This is their less-risky ticket into real estate investing. They provide money for rentals, escrow, fix-and-flips, and everything in between. Beyond providing the money, they have little to do except receive passive income in the form of repayment and interest. They also get better returns than most other investments, especially when you factor in the low risk of real estate. This is because you're investing in something that you can see, smell, and touch; you can visit the property, so you know where your money is located rather than when you're investing in stocks, or somebody's start-up company.

The most important thing when you're investing money is to understand the downside of the opportunity. Let's say the market completely crashes. Does your lender have the ability to get their money out of it? The answer is yes. Even when the market completely crashes, rental rates historically go up. People need to live somewhere, whether or not they can afford a home. Real estate is the safest thing ever. You get money every thirty days like clockwork.

When you're borrowing money from someone, you want to work with an attorney or a title company because you want everything to be legal. You want to be protected and you want the investor to be protected. You're building a relationship with an investor, not just trying to do one big deal or one quick job. When you're borrowing money, you sign what's called a promissory note. The note will basically say that you promise to pay back the principal sum in installments at specific dates at a percentage and rate of return that was agreed upon. For a $60,000 loan, you may agree to an interest rate of 10 percent. When you do fix-and-flips, the monthly payments are only on the interest, and then you pay back the full amount by the given date. There's also writing in the document about late payments which might impose something like a $100 fine in addition to the payment.

In addition to the promissory note, you will also need to create a deed of trust, which is essentially a mortgage. If you're using a private money lender, then you can think of that person as the bank. In this case, the lender gets a deed of trust that guarantees their investment. When you borrow money from a bank, they give you a mortgage (whether you use a deed of trust or a mortgage when borrowing from a bank depends on which state you're in).

Then you record the deed of trust and the promissory note in the county recorder's office because, again, you want to make sure everything is secure. From the investor's point of view, they're now ensured that if you don't make payments in a timely manner, they get the house. The property is indebted to the lender if payments aren't made by the agreed-upon date. The property can't be sold and it can't be financed. You can't do anything with it without talking to the lender about it. The public record should also show what percentage is owed and what payments have been made.

You also need to get a set of recorded documents and a secured position on the property. This is basically a lien on the house. A lien is a legal claim against a property that can be used to collect a debt. You can put different people in different positions to make sure everyone is in a secure place to make the deal go through. This goes into the weeds a little, so talk with an attorney or escrow officer who understands liens as you create secondary positions and more complex situations.

Finally, I like to give my lender something I call a lender's policy. This is from the title company and provides insurance on all of the documents from the escrow company. It's the final piece of the puzzle of making sure the lender understands they're covered. It confirms that if anything happens to the property, the lender gets paid out of the lender's policy. It's insurance for the lender. We had a situation on a past deal where the escrow officer made a mistake on the paperwork, and because we bought $400 in insurance, the title company had to pay the lender their $85,000 back.

It took me ten years to learn all of this, so you just saved yourself a decade and a lot of headaches by reading this passage.

Securing Private Money

The key to getting private lender money is to sound professional, whether you're a newbie or a veteran. You don't need to necessarily be an expert, but you do need to understand basic terms like "interest rates," "points," "penalties," and "due dates."

First, break down the information for the lender. After you secure a deal, it's time to present the deal to the private lender. If you can confirm the deal is a good deal, with proven information, it's more likely the lender will fund it. Consider things like number breakdowns (purchase price, rehab costs, completion time), comps for the ARV, "before" pictures of the property, and an estimated closing date. If you're brand-new, just take your time with the pitch. You need to cross your T's and dot your I's, like you're about to appear on *Shark Tank*. Be confident and present the deal.

After you get contact information from a lender (including name, email, and cell phone number), consider the following questions as every lender can be different.

- Do you lend in my state?
- What is your LTV (loan-to-value ratio)?
- What is your CTV (capital-to-value ratio)?
- Do you provide rehab funds?
- Is there a draw inspection fee?
- How are draws handled?
- What is the interest rate?
- Are payments amortized or interest only?
- Do you charge points? If so, how many? Up front or at the end?
- Are there any other fees I should be aware of?
- What is the length of the loan?
- Do you allow extensions? Are there fees for extensions?
- How much notice will you need in order to close?
- Can you provide proof of funds if required? What is the process to get proof of funds?
- How long are these terms good for?
- Can we get the terms in writing?
- How many deals will you fund at one time?

- Is there a process to get better lending rates in the future?
- What is the procedure to present a deal?

These are standard questions, so feel free to adjust based on your business model.

After your private lender has agreed to the deal, it's time to draft up the paperwork. Make sure to include the promissory note and the mortgage or deed of trust, depending on which state your deal is in. Once the paperwork has been approved, sign and notarize the documents and quickly send them back to the private lender.

At this point, you need to close on the original purchase. At the closing, the private lender should be given a copy of the closing/settlement statement, wiring instructions for the actual money, and an insurance certificate regarding the deal. Then the private lender will wire the funds for the purchase to the title company on the day of the closing. This company records the mortgage or deed with the county and sends a copy back to the lender.

If you're doing a fix-and-flip, this is when you start the actual renovation. The rehab will be funded in draws (payments taken for construction) that are sent to the lender. The draws should include an itemized breakdown of completed work, images of completed work, and the amount of draw requested. If the private money lender is a debt investor and not an equity investor, each month an interest-only payment should also be made, based on a prorated balance plus draws.

Finally, you need to close on the sale. After the renovations have been completed and a retail buyer has been secured with a closing date scheduled, the private lender will provide a payoff letter. This letter will be created by the title company with principal amounts of the loan and any additional outstanding prorated interest on the deal. The title company sends the payoff proceeds directly to the private lender at the time of the closing so the private lender gets everything that was initially agreed upon. At this point, the lien is also released on the property.

When to Use Hard Money

In addition to private money from friends and family, there are hard money lenders. Hard money is not meant to be used for long-term financing. Instead, it's more of a bridge loan or short-term loan. The lender is there to provide a quick solution or help with a financial problem. The investor's goal is generally to get out as quickly as possible and quickly pay back the loan. A hard money lender is generally able to provide up to 70 percent of the ARV of the property. If the ARV is $100,000, for example, the hard money lender may be willing to provide up to $70,000 (you would, of course, be responsible for producing the remaining $30,000), but each case is different.

Interest rates on hard money loans are much higher than traditional loans. Hard money interest rates can be anywhere from 9–15 percent with an additional one to five points. The repayment period is also shorter, but it could be anywhere from a few months to a few years. For successful flippers, this is plenty of time to make a profit and pay back the lender. The setup provides security for all parties and can be beneficial for all.

Hard money loans are typically pursued by borrowers when a traditional loan is unavailable or simply doesn't fit the criteria they need for the deal. These types of loans are also beneficial for those who have bad credit, are self-employed, or are in any other situation where traditional financing is not available. A hard money loan is a great financial tool for anyone who has dealt with bad credit, a bankruptcy, difficult-to-verify income, or excessive debt. Investors starting out also need types of nontraditional lending such as a hard money loan. Many real estate investors use hard money because it's a quick way to raise money to make more money. Hard money loans are great for properties that are undeveloped or in need of short-term financing. They can be used for commercial and residential real estate transactions.

Where do you get a hard money loan? For real estate flippers, hard money is readily available. There are nationwide lenders in every single state and local lenders willing to provide hard money to real estate investors. The best way to find a reliable hard money lender is to reach out to other investors in my Facebook community or within the BiggerPockets community and see who they recommend and why. Even easier is to simply go to biggerpockets.com/loans to find and connect with BiggerPockets-vetted, investor-friendly lenders.

HOW TO APPLY FOR HARD MONEY

First, find a convincing real estate investment. In order to apply for a hard money loan, you need to have an investment for lenders to examine. If you're not convinced the investment will yield profits, then you surely won't be able to convince someone else to give you a loan. Find a deal, do your homework, and present the deal to a potential creditor. Use a formula like the one below for initial groundwork.

70 percent of ARV – Expenses and Repairs = Purchase Price

If a home could be worth $100,000 and you know it will take $20,000 in repairs, then you know you shouldn't spend more than $50,000 on the house and still make a profit.

Once you've found the investment, find a reliable hard money lender. There are a lot of scams out there, so be sure to vet and do your homework on a lender before you enter into a business relationship with one. Once you've found a lender, you need to figure out what their requirements are. Then you can write an executive summary and an exit strategy. An executive summary is just a summary of the investment you hope to make and includes the hard money loan. For this, remember to keep it short, but include necessary details. A single paragraph may be enough. Don't write a novel. You want to include:

- The amount of the needed loan.
- A reason for borrowing the money.
- The timeline for the investment. For the timeline, you will need to know how long it will take to repair and sell the property. There are ballpark figures, but it will depend on your crew and market.
- List your exit strategy. What will you do if you can't sell the house? Be clear in your exit strategy and backup plan.

Once you have your brief and informative executive summary written, next you'll need to fill out the hard money loan application. Make sure you do not skip over any relevant information. It's a hassle to resubmit a form and it makes you look unprofessional. Avoid this at all costs. With the application, include a comparable markets analysis (CMA), which contains comparable properties to confirm your hypothesis about the ARV of the house. Send your comps to the lender and make sure to include lots of pictures of the actual property, along with info on the overall neighborhood. Ask the lender how they wish to receive these documents (some prefer online while other old-school investors may want a printout).

You should also include a detailed repair breakdown, especially if you're planning to rehab the property. Get bids from local contractors and take the average for the price and the timeline.

Next, back up the loan. Traditional lenders will want to see a good credit score, but hard money lenders are more concerned with the prospective deal than the individual making the deal. If the deal meets their LTV, it should get approved. That said, you may still need to provide a list of assets or other forms of confirmation that you are creditworthy. This could be cash. This could be other real estate properties. If nothing else, the lender needs to know you can pay holding costs. Experience and credit history are also important as your business grows.

Finally, submit your documents and start to build trust. When you complete all needed repairs, organize them and submit them to the lender so you can keep in touch throughout the process. Let them know their money is in good hands and you're reliable. This is a good first step in building trust for future projects. Be sure to answer or return calls promptly. Check your emails and text messages. Building trust is vital not only for an individual project but also for your long-term goals. Real estate, after all, is about building relationships. Once you've done these steps, you'll find that hard money loans help you close fast, and it's not necessary to have perfect credit to close big deals.

If you're hesitant about this type of deal, take some more time on your math to make sure it works and think about long-term deal strategy, not just a single deal. You're building a business, not selling snake oil. Don't worry about the interest rate. Yes, 9–15 percent sounds high, but it's the cost of doing business. Hard money loans are about closing fast and doing multiple deals. If the math works, it works. Then get prequalified. Getting prequalified is the best way to get cash fast. Learn what the lenders are looking for and present deals within their criteria. After you're pre-approved, build a solid relationship with local lenders. The quickest way to build your business is to build solid relationships. Don't limit yourself with one lender. Give yourself options.

For more peace of mind, determine the lender's prepayment penalty. Always learn the worst-case scenario, because things happen on job sites. The penalty is usually a percentage of the outstanding balance. Ask questions. Don't be afraid to learn everything you need to know about the deal. Hard money lenders will provide as much as you want to borrow, but you need to know what deals they're interested in. All hard money lenders have a sweet spot in which they prefer to do deals, so ask questions and get to know your lender to make their short list. I know this can sound like a lot to juggle, but the more you repeat these processes and questions, the easier it will get. Over time, the tasks that seem overwhelming in the beginning will become second nature, and you will forget that there was a time that you didn't know any of this.

For your deal, never misrepresent a property. The value is the value, but it can be tempting to misrepresent it in collateral-based lending. Don't do it. You will regret it. This might mean being more honest with yourself about the deal. Then ensure the property is competitive. Like comping, know that your property is competing with other properties in the market. An uncompetitive property is difficult to sell, so make your deal stand out.

This is the time to start building a network. Just like any good business, your business is built on solid relationships. Build a network of reliable people to close deals faster and more often. Success is not a secret. It's a grind. Do all the small steps so the big steps fall into place.

INVESTOR STORY
David Gulick—Seller Finance Wraps
"Grow into your niche business."

David Gulick, aka Medium Wave Dave, does deals in the Hamptons and the Southeast. Originally they were heavy direct-to-seller, but he's had several businesses in my mentorship and feels like he's in his fifth business, with a heavy focus on Joint Venture (JV). By putting himself out there, he gets a lot of JV deals from new people. He sees his role in the business as simply being visible and then showcasing his system to talk to people, which he mainly does through Instagram.

In this deal, a wholesaler brought him an auction deal, but there was a high entry fee. David has found this weeds out a lot of amateurs, so he looks for those types of deals. Because he's known in the community, it's easier for him to raise private capital. He can say yes to things that most people have to say no to. This was one of those deals.

The wholesaler's deal was a $306,000 hybrid. It had decent equity, but also arrears. The ARV was about $445,000 and the underwriting first was $186,000 with 2 percent interest. There was about $100,000 in arrears that got negotiated down to $70,000. The seller wanted $70,000 with $20,000 down, and that meant they would seller-finance the other $50,000 at zero percent interest and a five-year balloon. David had to do all of this four days before auction and the seller was also in the military, so they had a lot riding on it.

David had to pay $15,000 to the wholesaler, $20,000 to the seller, and then around $5,000 in closing costs, so that plus the auction was a $120,000 entry fee. Originally, he wanted to keep the house, but the entry fee was so high that he then planned to retail the house. But the tenant who had stayed in the house before did a number on the place, so he then had to renegotiate the deal. David gave extra money down and paid everyone else a little more money, but then felt more risk based on the renovation cost, so he was afraid he'd lose money in the end.

David set up risk on the back end. He promised the seller a $10,000 kicker if he made over $20,000 in profit. This way, they insulated the risk, helped out the seller, and everyone could get paid without losing their shirt or the private lender's capital. Moving the money to the back end allowed Dave to offer the seller a portion of the profits rather than paying on the front end.

David listed the house for $425,000 and got no response. He dropped the price two weeks later and decided to find a local Realtor. The Realtor gave him some insight on the market. He learned that anything over $400,000 in that area wasn't taken seriously without a Realtor on the deal. In this case, David decided to wrap the deal, cash out the private money, and sit on the second note to a note investor with a little over $500-per-month cash flow and no skin in the game. David will then list with this Realtor and sell for $425,000 total.

⚷ KEY TAKEAWAY | As you grow in the business, you can find niche areas to focus on deals where there's less or no competition. Then, once your bills are paid, the business becomes a game.

CHAPTER 13

The Legal Side of Subject-To

"People will love you and support you when it's beneficial."

—NICKI MINAJ, "PILLS N POTIONS"

Some of you bought the book for this chapter. Some of you are going to skip over it entirely. I'll start by repeating the fact that I'm not an attorney nor am I an accountant. I'm just following a path and sharing my story so you can do the same. Now that we got that disclaimer out of the way again, let's break down legal issues and misconceptions.

There's a challenge in doing deals all over the country. Even my team gets a little overwhelmed thinking about the many regulations and issues within real estate. As we learn new things, we add new clauses and new addenda to help us out with unusual seller situations. For example, in a deal we were working on in Vegas, we found out the seller hadn't paid their mortgage for a few months. We were under contract, so they thought we were supposed to be paying even though they were still living in the property. Just a weird, foolish misunderstanding. We have to add little addenda for all sorts of things like this, which is why we're constantly updating our contracts and working to protect ourselves in all sorts of deals.

Our team specifically works with a local attorney named Sean St. Clair, who specializes in real estate, business, and estate planning in the Arizona market. Sean occasionally hops on calls with our team so new investors can ask questions and learn more about any unique investment situations and how to handle them legally. He's an expert in fair housing, real estate agent laws, civil complaints, real estate contracts and deeds, and anything else we might need to know to do any individual deal.

He's able to create paperwork for our team that includes:

- Wholesale purchase contracts.
- Subject-to purchase contracts.
- Wrap agreements.
- Subject-to addenda.
- Options to purchase.
- Assignments.
- Joint Venture agreements.
- Substitution of collateral clauses.
- Notes.
- Deeds of trust.
- Residential lease agreements.

You can find a lot of these contracts on my website, and they're constantly being updated as we make important changes. Let's begin with the due-on-sale clause, which is, in regard to subject-to, my bread-and-butter closer.

Due-on-Sale Clause

What about the due-on-sale clause? This is one of the most common questions and concerns I see on social media regarding seller financing. What's the due-on-sale clause and how do you avoid it? There are four main ways the due-on-sale clause gets called on when you do a seller finance deal. When I say called on, I'm talking about buying a property subject-to when the original bank decides they want all their money up front, meaning it's due on sale.

How does this happen? There's failure of paperwork on the insurance side, meaning the seller cancels the insurance early. They have to keep this in place for a short duration even after you close escrow. Within a few months, you should replace the policy with a new one. Here you can trigger the clause again if you don't do the paperwork correctly for the new insurance. The majority of due-on-sale clause activations happen in this scenario.

The next trigger is when the seller wants more money before close of escrow. An angry seller can call you and demand more money. I had a seller threaten me by saying, "I'm going to call the bank and tell them what you're doing if I don't get an extra $10,000." In this case, he was referring to the due-on-sale clause, which is easily avoidable (read more about this later in the book), but I told him I wanted to cancel the contract, because I didn't want this threat looming over me. He said he would not go through with it and we kept the contract in place, but three months later, he did call the bank to get the property back. The way we work around this now is that we have our attorneys create a document saying that if the seller ever tampers with the mortgage or insurance, they get a $50,000 judgment put against their name. Having sellers sign off on this protects us from this scenario. We haven't had this happen again since that issue. In that case, we called the bank and they decided to let the note stay in place despite the angry seller threatening us.

Next, and perhaps most obvious, there's default in payment to the mortgage company. If you default on payment, the mortgage company is going to find out what's going on during the foreclosure process. If you buy a property that you can't afford, you should give it back to the owner. That's the right thing to do. However, if the servicing is not done correctly, meaning the servicing company failed to let them know the mortgage company sold to another mortgage company and therefore the payment location changed, or something similar, you can also lose the property. This is why you need a good servicing company and you need monthly reports and receipts to make sure no errors are made.

Finally, there's the possibility of facing an issue with small banks. If you buy a mortgage in a bank with five branches or fewer, the owner of the mortgage will notice ownership transfer. If this is the case, I would suggest you buy the property on an agreement for sale rather than subject-to so you have equity but not a fee title. This is just a good way to avoid this complication, which is common with smaller banks.

To avoid these due-on-sale issues entirely, make sure you set everything up properly. Make sure you are transparent with the seller and even have the insurance person call the seller to make sure everything is clear. Then set up your servicing properly so you get a report and receipt every month like clockwork. You also need to structure the entity where the owners of the LLC are hidden. I buy in a family trust to avoid my name being on the documents for safety and security reasons. Finally, you should put equity insurance on the property. This confirms that you are secure if the due-on-sale clause is pushed. They basically refinance the mortgage to you, and then you pay the insurance company rather than the bank that called the due-on-sale clause into order.

Up-to-Date Contracts

A lot of people don't know where to get a contract, so I provide those for you online. But if you're using contracts you downloaded from me two years ago, they're out of date. I constantly provide free contracts online that are worth thousands, if not tens of thousands, of dollars in lawyer fees, but make sure you always have the most recent contracts. My team is constantly finding new ways to protect ourselves and new ways to protect sellers and our contracts reflect these changes. People need to make sure they have the proper contracts. We work constantly on our contracts and they're always evolving.

I recently spoke with investor Jerry Norton and he even said he felt his contracts from last year had "too much teeth in his favor," meaning if they were to go to court, he could potentially lose if the judge didn't agree with the initial documentation. Essentially, he wanted for things to be fairer for both parties. You want to protect yourself, but you don't want to show up with a biased contract that makes you look one-sided in court.

An issue I recently ran across relates to filing a memorandum without consent of the seller. Technically, this is a misdemeanor, which means you won't go to prison, but you could get a fine. I just added a small paragraph in the contract that says my team can file a memorandum if we need to do so. We're getting in the weeds a little with this, but I just want to provide examples and encourage you to hire a creative finance attorney and a title company that understands your business and all current methods to better protect you and the seller when you do deals.

In an ideal world, we would all use a universal contract, but currently this isn't the case. For now, to begin with, I think all contracts should clearly disclose your plans to the seller. If you're going to assign the contract, you should have a section that says you may assign the contract to another LLC. You don't have to legally do that, but it's better to talk about this than try to hide it or do something where it's a problem later. It's fine to say you don't know exactly what you're going to do with the property. You can say, "This might be a rental. This might be an Airbnb. This might be a fix-and-flip," but those strategies should all be listed in the paperwork as you figure out your exit strategy during the inspection phase as you close the deal. The disclosure is just saying that you intend to profit in this transaction and there are multiple paths to make a profit.

A few years ago, I didn't disclose the fact that I planned to make money on a deal when I was buying a house from a veteran (even though this should have been obvious), and I didn't have any language in the contract that said I didn't coerce or manipulate the seller. A week later, when a wholesaler offered them more money, the veteran called and said they were not going to sell the property and were going to stay in the house. When I called my attorney to see if the paperwork would hold up in court, he told me I didn't have this language listed, so, if we did go to court, the veteran could go to the news, and it would be a negative story about me, to say the least. Lesson learned. I made sure to add the profit disclosure. The same is true for earnest money—a security deposit made at the date of the initial transaction—even if it's just $1, list it on the document. Everything needs to be there. It's protection for you and earnest money confirms that you legally plan to go through with the contract.

This earnest money exchange changes state by state, so talk to your attorney about how to work around this. I've got $1,000 sitting in a title company in Texas because the seller never agreed to release the money back to me. Everything was legal, but the seller didn't sign off on the deal after I backed out, so the money is stuck there essentially for all of eternity (he won, I guess).

Sitting Down with a Seller

In one particular live session with my students, we went over a contract with my attorney to talk about how to properly fill out a contract with a seller. Simply start at the top and take your time to figure out the individual steps so you fill out the contract in its entirety.

Start with describing the property. The legal description is the most important part as sometimes the address changes, but the legal description does not change. In my current document, this is on the first page. An attorney may tell you to pull the legal description from the most recent deed.

Then go through the individual document and fill out all the information and make sure the seller is on board with each aspect of the deal. Again, your job is to educate, not just to close the deal. Confirm the information from the seller is correct. Talk about the purchase price again. Write down the earnest money. Discuss the existing mortgage. Discuss a potential second mortgage. Discuss the possibility of another loan to the buyer. The seller is going to have to initial or sign each page.

You will also need to include:
- The close of escrow.
- The seller carryback financing (allows seller to become the lender).
- The escrow agents.
- The inspection period.
- The total purchase price.
- Any associations.
- Specific closing costs, and how those closing costs are to be broken up.

In the end, this isn't the sexiest part of closing a deal, but it's certainly a major part. That's why you need to hire an attorney who understands your business model in the state you are making the deal. Then make sure you understand all aspects of the contract so you can better explain the contract to the seller. Also, since it's different state by state, make sure any paperwork you download online fits the criteria you're looking for with your particular deal. Protect yourself. Take your time. Hire a professional who has your best interest in mind.

INVESTOR STORY
Caleb Christopher—Creative Closer
Case Study
"Keep the House in Your Family's Name . . ."

Caleb Christopher loves listening to stories. Before getting into real estate, he worked in a prison where he would talk with inmates about their stories. In this case study, Caleb was working as a lead manager and creative closer for a mastermind student before he started his own business.

In this scenario, two brothers lost their mom, and probate was wrapping up, so they were required to sell the house. One brother was listed on the title, but neither one of them—nor the duo together—could afford to buy the title. They had to sell.

They grew up there and wanted to keep the house for sentimental reasons. One brother was living there and had two kids and two dogs but couldn't afford to buy the house. He went through the process with the banks and got an appraisal for $138,000, but the banks wouldn't touch it because he had just changed jobs. This is where a creative closer comes in.

I know many new investors who work part-time in the business as they learn different aspects of the deal flow. This lead came from a cold call—their number was on either a foreclosure list or something similar—and they needed a creative solution since the banks wouldn't help them out and the parents didn't put an estate plan together. This goes to probate, which is how the state clears out the estate.

This is a tough situation for the family to be in, but as a creative closer, you can solve this. It's all about the numbers and the terms of the deal. Here's what happened. Caleb got to know their story. They had already rejected a cash offer so they needed a creative solution. He told them, "I want to keep you in this house. Let's find a way to do that."

The appraisal was fewer than thirty days old, which meant Caleb could ask for a specific discount to get a loan on the house. In this case, it was a $95,000 loan with 8 percent interest (this included a $10,000 assignment fee for the wholesaler who brought in the lead, so the offer to the brothers was $85,000). Then Caleb could lease the brother the house back. This meant working out a deal where their lender would give them 100 percent of the value for the house, which is unheard of because there's no insulation for the risk.

Caleb also created a five-year option to buy the house back. He wanted to get it 100 percent financed, then lease it back with an option to purchase. Then, as long as Caleb was the first owner, he would let them have thirty days' right of refusal to purchase after the five-year period. He also showed them all of the numbers, so he could work out a discount and make the terms so he'd make a little money each month. They agreed to the deal and were even somewhat excited about it.

This worked because the main goal was to keep the house in the family's name. This was their bunnies. Caleb paid the lender about $800 per month and he brought in $1,300 per month so there was a cash flow cushion for repairs and so he could make some money on the deal. The brothers were going from paying virtually $0 per month to $1,300 per month, but they had a clear set of pain points and a creative solution was the only way this could work out for them. This deal was $0 out of pocket and worked out for everyone.

Caleb insisted on owning the property so he could get the loan in full. This meant the brother had to be a renter for a period of time to protect the deal. He told them it was going to be an unfair number and they should take a cash deal. But, because of the sentimental value of the property, they were in for the lower deal. They agreed to $85,000. Then, two days before closing, the lender called and said he would drop to 6 percent instead of 8 percent. Now instead of $600 per month, Caleb only had to pay $400 per month. This last-second change meant he could make more money per month. Also, Caleb had already factored in potential expenses including a management fee, which he paid himself in this scenario. He also chose not to ask for an up-front fee, which most lease deals include.

It's somewhat risky to rent back to the owner. Typically, you don't want to wrap the property and sell it back to the owner. Those sentimental, emotional issues can make waves in the property. If they were paying $700 per month and now you need them to pay $1,400 per month, it's natural that they can have some animosity. It can be problematic, but owning real estate with tenants in it is problematic in nature.

Months later, Caleb was making money from the deal and the brother was happy. Again, the brother had a good job and was only denied because he had recently moved from one employer to another employer, although it was in the same field. Caleb also allowed for the tenant to improve the house as long as there was written approval. This included new doors and similar changes. The deal they set up allowed for the brother to buy the house at $125,000, which was still a discount from the appraisal. Caleb set up percentage increases of $131,250 after twenty-four months, then $144,375, and so on as the options were ongoing. The longer the brother took to buy it, the more money Caleb would make. In the end, Caleb cash flowed about $400 per month and knew he would make at least $30,000 when the brother did choose to buy the house back.

KEY TAKEAWAY | Caleb didn't let his nine-to-five get in the way of entering the business and he wasn't too proud to work with another investor to turn this "dead lead" into a profitable solution. Wholesalers want low-hanging fruit, but if you try just a little harder, you can find big money.

CHAPTER 14

Paperwork and Flow of the Deal

"I sell ice in the winter, I sell fire in hell / I am a hustler baby, I'll sell water to a well."

—JAY-Z, "U DON'T KNOW"

The Traditional (Retail) Sale

Understanding a retail sale is super important because you need to know how each party makes money for you to make money. In this particular flow, everything gravitates around the buyer. What do they want? What do they need? What are they willing to pay? What will the house appraise for? It all circles around these questions and the buyer's state of mind. Without this end answer, you can't build a formula for everyone else to get paid. It's all about the buyer and the seller.

The seller is ready to sell a property, so let's say they hire a listing agent to list it on the MLS. The buyer's agent goes out and looks for properties within the buyer's criteria. Once they find one, they submit it to the buyer. If the buyer likes it, they submit an offer on the home. The listing agent then goes back and forth with the buyer's agent until they agree upon a price in a document known as the purchase price contract. This is the agreement between the buyer and the seller. This goes to either the title company or a local attorney. It's the instructions for how everyone should handle the deal. They're also confirming there are no liens or anything that could wreck the deal. Then escrow begins on the property for a period of time. At this point, they decide on the COE, or close-of-escrow date. All parties involved need to get to work so the buyer can take over the property on this date.

Outside the buyer, the seller, and the title company, there's a lender and underwriter who verifies that the buyer fits the parameter of the lender's guidelines. They send over loan documents and a clear-to-close statement, which means the funds have been proven. Then the buyer sends an inspector over to make sure the property is safe and there are no issues: This could include anything from termites to fire safety concerns. An inspector costs between $300 and $600 nationwide.

Once the inspector is called in and does their job, they send over their list of things to look at. This may require items to be repaired or a credit to be added to the document. Sometimes it's something small like adding a handrail to a staircase, repairing termite damage, or addressing an out-of-date maintenance problem. If there's a list of repairs, that list can go to a contractor and then the contractor confirms with the inspector. Once everyone agrees with everything, they can move forward. But, before closing, the appraiser comes in and confirms that the lender is lending an amount of money that makes sense. This is particularly important in hot housing markets. Some people are overpaying $25,000 or $50,000. Even if the homeowner is willing to pay more than the home is worth, this could put the lender in a bad situation; they don't want to over-lend for the deal. The appraiser is on the seller's side and they have to make sure it meets the lender's guidelines. This is less important in an all-cash deal.

There are all sorts of variables, but this is the basic flow of a retail (aka traditional) deal.

Traditional versus Creative

Most people only understand conventional financing. Everybody thinks this is how it should be done. Buying a house is a big deal, right? You should need to talk to a bank and have two years of pay stubs and all of this other nonsense, right?

The majority of the acquisitions you will learn from me are subject-to or seller financing or some hybrid model. But first, let's break down traditional financing. With traditional financing, you need:

- A social security check.
- A credit check.
- A down payment.
- A job history.
- Enough time to deal with this long, exhaustive process.

A lot of people can't buy a house because they don't have the right credit. They don't have bad credit, but they also don't have good credit. One of the long-term consequences of the 2008 real estate crash was a major change in mortgage lending policies. Gone are the days of borrowers with low or no credit scores getting approved by traditional lenders for home loans.

The lender tells you to go out and get some credit cards and then, in a year or two, the bank will grant you the right to buy a house. Then the bank qualifies you; that means you have a lender that will lend you a specific amount of money. At this point, you can go out and find a house that fits this criterion. This may be how your parents bought a house. This may be how most of your friends bought a house.

But that's merely the beginning. Now the lender has to underwrite your property. They have to ask you about every little thing in your life. This is painful for people. It's exhausting. They need tax returns for the past two years. They need to call previous employers. They need to pull your credit (again). Week in and week out, they examine you with a magnifying glass and it's just generally a pain. I would say about one-third of people who apply are automatically denied, and then another 20 percent who get prequalified experience deals that fall apart once they get them under the magnifying glass. Then the loan falls apart and the lenders walk away. This is how people think a property needs to be purchased. This is how people buy personal houses.

Ironically, lenders are even worse when you want to buy an investment property. They may only give you 65 percent of the total instead of 80 percent, which means you need more money to put down. It's super challenging to build a rental portfolio with traditional financing. It's a little less complicated with fix-and-flips, because hard money lenders are only concerned with the assets themselves. Creative finance is generally a better solution for long-term investors.

Where does the money come from with creative finance? You can utilize someone else's credit on a loan that was confirmed years earlier and there's no limit to how many houses you can buy. (You can only get thirteen traditional loans at one time no matter how good your credit is and no matter how much money you have in the bank.) All of my rental properties come from somebody else's credit that I didn't have to qualify for. I have no limit on how many houses I can buy. I simply put myself in a position where I can utilize someone else's loans legally. With creative finance, you can control real estate without using any of your own money or any of your credit. This is the path to generational wealth. This is how you build a legacy.

In the beginning of the book, I wrote about meeting an escrow agent/angel in disguise named Eileen. Eileen taught me the fundamental steps to get started in real estate as an investor. As a reminder, she told me to go out there and make some problems and then bring her those problems. It was such a unique position to be in. She knew my strengths and she knew my weaknesses. She knew I could put my head down and grind it out, but she also knew I was in the beginning of my career and didn't have the knowledge it took her forty years to acquire. I don't know that she intended to be my mentor, but that's what she was. Remember, a good mentor is an important part of your investor tool kit. A good mentor can cut years (and costs) off your learning curve, and this is true for any new business venture you undertake. Not everything can be learned on YouTube. Eileen told me to go out there and learn by doing. And that's exactly what I teach investors. If you're serious about this business, you have to be willing to take action and make some mistakes. It's the only way to learn and, therefore, the only way to grow.

This is how I operate on a daily basis. It's all about learning enough to take action, and then taking action. People who scroll all day and search all day to figure out every little aspect rarely make progress. This is because people like to solve problems they don't even have. What will I do if I get too many houses? What will I do if I land a big deal but there's a problem I've never read about? You have to learn by doing, not obsessing and doing nothing. It's why I get up early. It's why I work weekends. I want to learn, put the new ideas into action, fail, repeat, and grow. Information put into practice is information that you are later able to utilize and turn into a superpower. If you're going to be successful in this business, it's ideal that the people you work with—like title and escrow officers and closing attorneys—are willing to help you grow and teach you along the way as you bring them profitable problems.

The Right Escrow Officer

Finding the right escrow officer or closing attorney can be a way to find the best member of your team. It's not just another spoke in the wheel. First, I want to clarify something. A lot of people say title officer and escrow officer interchangeably, but they're two different things. An escrow officer handles the transaction from when it starts to when it finishes. A title company makes sure the transaction is handled properly, and they also insure the transaction. The title company makes sure there are no problems with the property while it's going through escrow, clouded titles (meaning an irregularity on a title document), and so on. We do talk about title and escrow somewhat interchangeably, but they are two different things. In terms of title and escrow, opening escrow is the beginning of the transaction, where closing escrow is the end of a transaction. If you hear someone say they're in escrow, they're in the middle of a transaction.

For now, I want to focus on people who help you close, which would be the escrow officer, the closing attorney, or a title officer. What are characteristics of a great title officer? What are the attributes you should look for? What should you avoid? I've had some really good title officers and some really bad title officers. The problem with a bad title officer is obvious, but the problem with a good title officer is that sometimes they get too good and have to turn away business. They can't handle all the files. They're so successful they experience what tech people call the "hug of death," which means they're overbooked and unavailable.

Where I like to start is by researching local title companies and then reaching out to other investors to see who they are using. You can basically create an informal poll to see who is good and who is not good. If you're in the business for a few years, it's possible a good title agent will become overbooked and then you need to reach out and find other title companies again through your network. Success brings problems, but you're a problem solver, so this is nothing to worry about.

CREATIVE FINANCE EXPERTS

First and foremost, a title officer needs to understand how the elements of creative finance work in the first place. They need to be comfortable with subject-to, with seller finance, with assignments, with double closes, with notes, with wraps. I cannot stress the importance of this. That's why it's a good idea to ask for recommendations from other investors. You know a recommended title agent understands the terms because they're currently active in the field. You don't want to waste time having to educate title companies that don't understand what you're doing. There's not a state in the country that hasn't dealt with some form of creative finance, so you need to find educated people who can help you with your deals. This doesn't mean you can't learn from one another, but you don't want to start with someone who has no idea what you're trying to accomplish. That's a surefire path to failure and big mistakes. Every state has thousands of these transactions every year. You just need to find a title company that can handle these types of deals.

In addition to already working with investors, your title company needs to be highly responsive. This is the difference between mediocre and excellent. An excellent title company is there when you need them. If your officer is too busy, they should have a system in place so you can at least get in touch with someone else in the office. They should get back to you in a quick manner and answer the phone when you call. They should also provide national lead lists. My title company provides leads for me at no charge. They also put on investor meetups to help me connect with other investors in my local market. This is how you get deals done and raise money and expand your business. It's always better to collaborate than it is to compete. You're probably going to be doing a little bit of both, but be open to creating win-win scenarios; you can go faster alone, but you can go further together.

I recently attended a meetup where my title officer spent over $1,000 on food and beverages just to put on a good networking event for local investors. This title company understands the importance of doing good business and they're constantly raising the bar and surpassing my expectations. How do you find your own title company? Talk to investors, of course, but if you're brand-new and don't know investors in your area yet, check on local real estate Facebook groups, check on Google Maps, look for referrals on social media, and ask about local title companies on the BiggerPockets forums. Find someone who is using a title company they like. You can also reach out to my team and see who we've used in any state. Some title companies also do virtual real estate transactions, so you can use them in multiple states and know they're going to do a good job for you.

After you find a few potential title companies to call, have a conversation with them. Ask if they have any escrow officers who specialize in investment files. Tell them what types of deals you do, like seller finance and subject-to and assignments. Ask if you can connect to have a conversation about what they can do for your business.

"Hello, I'm an investor in the _____ area and I primarily run a wholesale and creative finance business

model. I'm curious if you are familiar with this model or work with clients who run similar investment businesses in the area."

Show up with good questions and know what answers you expect to receive before you make the call. Then make a handful of calls to find the right officer for you.

FOLLOW-UP QUESTIONS

Be advised: In addition to you vetting them, they're vetting you. Not every title company wants to work with wholesalers. Everyone has their own preconceived notions and their own baggage. You're trying to see if this is a fit for you and they're doing the same thing. Some follow-up questions I like to ask include the following.

- Do you have multiple branches in the area?
- Can clients sign at any branch location?
- Are there lead lists or market materials you provide to investors?
- Do you host investor meetups or something similar?
- What does your fee structure look like?
- What type of investor discounts do you offer?
- Are there any additional disclosures that you do for subject-to, seller finance, double closes, or assignments?

You can also ask them to give you one page of another client's redacted recent HUD (a home purchased with a settlement; HUD refers to Housing and Urban Development), because there are more things than just closing costs to consider. There could be an HOA transfer fee, a rush fee, or a fee for a mobile notary, so you want to have those numbers up front in order to properly evaluate your deal. Hidden costs can kill your investment businesses, so take some time to learn everything you can up front. You will still make mistakes, but show up prepared and get all of the information you can as you start to do deals.

As you start to do some volume, there are other questions you can ask based on your scalability and everything else you're bringing to the table. In my business, I want to make sure my escrow officer has an assistant, because I know they're regularly in closings for multiple hours at a time, but I still need to get my emails answered quickly. Deals happen quickly, so your escrow officer needs to be reliable and have a system in place to be available, one way or another. I would also ask if they're going to be available to write up addenda and other things that I don't know exactly how to do in the proper manner. My title company does this all the time. They also talk to sellers for me and help me out when I don't have the time. Your title company is a business and they should serve you like a business. They're providing a service, not just providing plug-and-play answers for you.

There's a general assumption that title officers and escrow officers are somewhat stuffy or unapproachable. However, as I am sure you can imagine, these people are busy (especially in a real estate market like the one we have had in recent years) and have a lot on their plates. People assume they will not help you out, but that's not the case when you find the right company to work with. These title companies want your business. Post in a Facebook group, visit the BiggerPockets community, do a Google search, find referrals, and take the time to have a conversation with the title company or companies that best fit your criteria. Like all great relationships in life, sometimes it can take time to find the right one.

INVESTOR STORY
Jen Shelton—Seller Finance Sub-Tail
"Dream house in the middle of nowhere."

Jen Shelton lives in Southern California and she's been in the mentorship almost two years. She's a real estate investor and a Pilates instructor. You can watch some of her calls on her social media channels for more deal breakdowns and seller call tips. She also recently built a team around her business and her goal is to build a scalable team where she can start to take more time off to spend with family.

In one of her deals, she was trying a Facebook nationwide ad and found one good lead. They used a secondhand company for ad filtration, but only got one of seventy-five decent leads. It came from Deming, New Mexico. The problem with ads like this is that they can find you leads, but they're often leads in areas where it's difficult to find a buyer. They're smaller markets, so getting a contract isn't hard, but closing is the hardest part.

For the one that worked, the seller was willing to sell sub-to, zero down, zero interest, so it was hard to say no to the deal. It was nothing out of pocket except for $450 PITI. Jen described the property as "livable," so they closed on the deal and planned to simply replace the out-of-date appliances. But they couldn't find a title company in the area that did creative deals so they self-performed with Constant Close, an online company.

The seller said they had found their dream home in the country and bought it on terms. They were already familiar with seller finance, which meant they were open to selling their previous house on seller finance. They understood the terminology and also knew that since they just bought the first house a year earlier, they didn't have any equity and they didn't want to make double payments.

The transaction coordinator carried out the process rather than using a title company as there wasn't a title company to use. This used to be the normal thing. People would hand over a deed for money. This meant the transaction coordinator could work with the county clerk officer in New Mexico to transfer over the deed without the need of a title company. Jen ran the title to make sure there were no liens, but that was it. It cost around $1,000 to close out this deal.

At the time, Jen couldn't find anyone familiar with Deming, so she reached out to Realtors to see who might be investor friendly. She planned on owner financing, which meant it would be a wrap deal. Finally, she found an agent who owned properties himself and was comfortable selling on terms. He knew there was a market for terms and he was even willing to walk the property before the close. The day they closed the deal, he listed it. He listed it as a normal deal and got a traditional offer over asking price. Jen likely could have made more with seller financing, but since she got the opportunity for a high cash offer and she was new in the business, she took the high cash offer.

The mortgage was $96,000. She spent about $4,500 on appliances and mortgage payments during the sales process. In the end, she made a little over $23,000 on the deal from the sale, so she profited about $18,000 and felt like the deal worked out super well for everyone. Since she bought the house subject-to and sold it retail, this is considered a sub-tail deal. Thanks to the fact that she had these tools in her tool kit, she was able to make the deal work.

KEY TAKEAWAY | It's not a bad idea to try different marketing leads, but learn from your mistakes and always narrow your sales niche.

CHAPTER 15

Who Can Help Me Run My Business?

"Work hard for the money, but it ain't about cash.
Life's a schoolyard, I ain't gettin' picked last."

—**CHILDISH GAMBINO, "I'M A WINNER"**

You've got your structure. You've got your war chest. Now it's time to build your team. This is incredibly important for multiple reasons, but mainly because you can't build a legacy by yourself. It's impossible. Even my favorite examples—Michael Jordan, Steve Jobs, Rihanna—all had teams behind them. That's just how a legacy works.

Let's talk about your first hire and how you can allow your team to grow so you can grow. The challenge in writing about team building is that everyone reading this book is going to be in a different level of their business. That said, there are certain qualities to look for, certain pay structures to build out, a way to set up culture and growth promises, various types of software and communication to consider, ways to think about team management, and, of course, automation.

When you start any business, you wear a lot of hats. You have to do a little bit of everything, all by yourself, in order to go from zero to one. You have to figure out lead generation. You have to figure out lead conversion. You have to learn how to disposition a property. You have to learn about management and scaling. And, in reality, all of these hats are full-time jobs in themselves. It's complicated. It's complex. It's frustrating. But the rewards are bountiful. This is even more true as you learn to scale with a team. Plus, when it's time to hire, guess who does the hiring? You do. Another job. But here's the truth: There is no working smart until you work hard. Then you can start to take chunks of work off your plate. The ultimate goal is to work hard, delegate, and build out your team.

Your first hire should be a virtual assistant. If I could go back in time, I would have hired a VA right out of the gate. Don't hire a family member. Don't hire a friend. Most people do not understand what it takes to be an entrepreneur, so your old friends are not a good fit for your future business. They don't understand the extra hours it takes, and they don't understand the risk you are dealing with being an entrepreneur. You need to find a team made up of people who understand how to work hard. Your first hire should be a VA who can help you with lead generation. A VA can set up a system and run that system for you. If your VA is trained properly, they should be able to make cold calls for you. But, since you're starting out, you can also have your VA pull lists, skip-trace leads, search for properties, run comps, and build out a follow-up system. With your first hire, you need to decide what they are going to do and what you are going to do and make sure the roles work together seamlessly.

As such, your second hire should also be a VA. This person should help with cold-calling, run SMS management, help with ringless voice mails, and do follow-up calls. You should pay your first VA anywhere from $3.50–$13 per hour, depending on their level of training. Hands down, the higher-priced and better-trained VA is always worth the investment.

Your third hire should be an acquisition manager (AM). This person will help you do more deals. Hire someone local or remote—as long as they understand your KPIs and your team management, and they're open to working on commission only. They're getting leads from your first one or two VAs, and their job is to follow up on those leads and close deals. If this person is making about fifty calls per day, they should get about twenty good-quality conversations per day. I pay my AM about 20 percent of the deal, which is a fair price. If I do a deal and make a $30,000 assignment on that deal, then my AM makes $6,000 for his wholesale fee as his commission.

Likewise, your fourth hire should be a junior acquisition manager (JAM). This person should make about 12 percent of the deal based on commissions for following up with leads and closing deals. In this scenario, the JAM is hired by the AM, so the AM makes 8 percent when the JAM makes 12 percent. This is because you're putting the AM in charge of the JAM. They hire and fire whoever they work with and train them as a manager. The AM makes less per deal, but more overall as they're managing multiple JAMs. This is an eat-what-you-kill model. My teams don't do base pay. We're looking for closers who work on commission. That said, we do hire people who work part-time elsewhere, like part-time nurses or Uber drivers. We've had great luck hiring firefighters because they have several days off per week. We're also open to training people to fix-and-flip while they make calls and close deals. This way, they're not stressed out and can make good money on the side.

Next, for the fifth and sixth hires, I would hire two additional VAs and put them in charge of more cold calls and more cold texts. When you have an acquisition team, you need more leads. You have to up your game. You have to make sure you have a conveyor belt of leads to keep doing deals and keep growing as a company. The platforms I use allow for my team to send thousands of text messages per week and make hundreds of calls per day. It's fast. It's seamless. It's one of the best ways to bring in leads. We also work in multiple areas so we don't oversaturate any particular area at one time.

Now it's time to move from lead conversion to disposition. You need to learn to sell. My team has a disposition manager—your seventh hire—who is an X-ray technician two days per week and works for us five days per week. Again, he's a person who has a paycheck and health insurance elsewhere, so he's just here to make money doing dispo. Our disposition manager gets 9 percent of everything that gets sold with his guidance. He works with the AM and JAM to make sure they're getting deals. I would also recommend that you have your disposition manager reach out to local wholesalers and local real estate agents and develop relationships with those people. Tell them that your team has a solid buyers list and you can help them offload deals, particularly if those deals can involve creative finance or out-of-the-box thinking. With this business model, where you have seven employees, you should be able to close at least five deals per month. Beyond this, any additional positions, like an officer manager, will likely need a base pay, so it gets more expensive as you start to branch out after your seventh hire. In the end, you must decide where you can improve and delegate tasks.

Goal Setting in Creative Finance

Every week, my partners and I schedule a planning session with one main purpose: goal setting. Goals are incredibly important and to meet goals, it generally comes down to understanding your "why." I wrote more about this in an earlier chapter, but here's my seven-layers-deep "why" as an example to get you thinking about your own "why."

I want to spend quality time with my family and completely invest in them. This means being present when we're together and making sure we live an abundant life. I also want to buy a ranch in Flagstaff. This location is about two hours from me, and my dream is to own a hundred-acre ranch where I can take my family to live like Davy Crockett on the frontier with no cell phones, few worries, and a present mindset.

This brings me to my next "why," which would be the ability to live life without being attached to my cell phone. Some entrepreneurs call stretches of time offline "walkabouts," but the goal here is to build such an efficient team that I can go off-grid for a month or longer without my business falling apart. I have to learn how to delegate. I have to learn how to pass off responsibilities.

And finally, to complete the picture, I want to purchase a small plane to fly to and from this location so we don't have to spend so much time on the road and we can hop in the plane and go whenever we want. Hopefully, you can see a little more detail here in my "why" to further craft your own "why" and your own hhyperspecific vision of the future. Either way, really get into it. I think about the color of the house, the type of plane, and, when I watch a show like *Yellowstone*, I see myself exploring lands worth much more than money. We set goals to make these things happen. They aren't dreams. They're goals. Everything is within your grasp when you're focused on the path.

Since we may have similar "whys," let's start with a goal we probably have in common: monthly cash flow targets and passive income. I got into this business because I wanted to figure out a way to make a specific amount of money that I thought would solve all my problems and set me up to accomplish my "why" dream on a specific timeline. Early in my career, my initial goal was to earn a monthly net of $100,000 and I gave myself four years to complete this goal. To achieve something like this, I like to set a goal and then backtrack. That's the goal, now how do I accomplish it? What does it look like on paper? What's realistic and what's not? Which system or process will help me capture these results?

At the time, I knew I needed to add an additional $25,000 a year in monthly cash flow to hit this specific income. I also knew I'm the type of person who wants to go above and beyond, but it's good to have this baseline so you know exactly what you need to accomplish to capture your "why." If I can make $2,000 per month from a rental property over a four-year period, that leads to about $96,000 (which is about $100,000 so let's use this for simple mathematical purposes). Since I know each rental property nets me about $500 per month, then I know if I can buy four houses per month for twelve months, I can easily hit this initial goal. I got there a little faster, but I needed the guideline to get started.

For your own goal, start with the end in mind and plan backward from there to where you are now. Be hyperspecific about your "why" and equally specific about your goals to achieve your "why." Think of it like writing a movie. I'll use something most of us have seen for this example that also has a major twist (spoiler alert if you haven't watched this movie in the last twenty years). In *The Sixth Sense*, I'm positive the writer-director M. Night Shyamalan came up with the twist ending first. He knows Bruce Willis is dead the whole time, but how does he get there? How can he keep the audience from knowing? How can he make the movie re-watchable where it's different on the second viewing once you know the ending? He starts with the end, then thinks about the third act, second act, first act, and builds an outline. In your case, you're the screenwriter and the outline is your life. Will you accomplish this goal in a year? Two years? Five years? Generally speaking, I like to start with a variety of goals because accomplishing starter goals will help you accomplish greater goals.

Let's backtrack a little more. What does it take to buy four houses per month? For my team, at the time, we generally needed to contact about 200 hot leads. In this case, I'm referring to people who have unlisted properties and are at least open to having a conversation about selling their property. Of these 200 names that our acquisition team spoke to, we could generally close about four deals within a thirty- to sixty-day time frame. That's really it. Yes, some months were higher. Some months were lower. And our closing rates are much higher now because our team is constantly improving, but it's a good idea to work with what you have and build on it. That's how you reach your goals. You can set seemingly impossible goals, but you shouldn't set expectations you can't achieve. Find the sweet spot in the middle as you build up your skill set, your tool kit, and your connections, then use incoming data to know what you can accomplish with your skills and abilities. Your goals should grow with you, so take a minute to determine what you really want and what you believe you need to get there. Then focus on incremental steps to achieve these goals.

Scaling Your Portfolio

As you start thinking about scaling and building a portfolio, once again you're thinking big picture, so you're thinking about legacy. It's important to have a set of rules when you build out a portfolio. Originally, I thought I would buy as many doors as possible and just keep them all. If they cash flow, then hold them long term, right? Why not? But as I've advanced in the business, I've realized this simply isn't the case. There's a number of reasons as to why or why not, but I want to focus on the rules I've set in place for my portfolio so you can use these in your own business and create your own rules. I can go to a real estate investment club and talk to someone and they might have completely opposing opinions, but that doesn't mean I'm wrong and it doesn't mean that person is wrong. It's about your goals and your strategies.

First of all, make sure you have a strategy. As I mentioned earlier, if you don't want 1,000 versions of a deal, then you shouldn't even make that single deal. If, for whatever reason, it doesn't fit your flavor profile or your gut tells you not to make the deal, don't do it. I heard this idea years ago at a rental mastermind, and I thought it was brilliant. Back then, I would buy a property, and then let a friend live in the property. I thought I was doing my friends a favor, but then, three years later, I ended up evicting a friend who couldn't make a payment. Trying to be the good guy, I put myself in a bad situation. Why did I do this? Because I didn't have a strategy. I didn't have rules set in place for these types of things. Imagine having 1,000 friends in 1,000 properties. It would be a nightmare. I mean, one turned into a nightmare. The same thing might be true if you find a property next to a landfill or something else that makes it hard to rent. If you don't want 1,000 versions, don't do the deal. Even building a good portfolio is not okay for someone who can't handle headaches; you need to manage those headaches. If it's not long term, wholesale the deal and make a little money, but move on. People don't take pride in saying no to a deal, but you need to think long term when you build a portfolio.

Next, don't be desperate. Don't contract a house just to contract a house. It's a great feeling to own properties and grow your business, but if you get too greedy, you can lose your vision. In the early days, I would contract houses just to contract houses. Then, when it was time to manage the property, the property profile didn't sit well with me so I ended up selling the deal or renovating or wrapping to end buyers. When you set that number, that goal of one hundred doors or 1,000 doors or whatever it is, you can be blinded by the number. You have to occasionally stop, slow down, step back, and make sure you're fitting the flavor profile for your portfolio. Don't be desperate. Be focused.

Create a property profile. What does this mean? Think about these questions.

- Where do you want to own the property?
- What type of cash flow are you okay with?
- What type of property do you want to own?
- Do you care if there's equity in the deal?

For me, I'm less concerned with equity than cash flow. But if there's a ton of value with a low interest payment, it's equally beneficial. Some investors like to focus on $350-per-month cash flow while others are okay with smaller margins because they know the rent can go up the following year. As Brandon Turner recounts in *The Book on Investing in Real Estate with No (and Low) Money Down*, his initial approach was that any cash flow was beneficial as he was starting to grow his business. It's up to you and your financial war chest and what you're willing to do to build the portfolio. I ask myself the four questions above when I buy a property. I like visiting Texas or Florida regularly, so I like to visit my properties there. I don't visit Michigan, for example, so I don't do deals there. The same is true for certain parts of Arizona, but my main criterion for any long-term property profile is going to be cash flow.

Then think about effective property management. Because of my background, I do my own property management. I don't see it as a problem, and I don't want to put that extra money into someone else's pocket. But if you can close big deals with room to pay a property manager, or you simply don't want to manage properties, you need to figure this out before you start to scale. In my first year of building a portfolio, I basically had to sell off a lot of my properties and start over from scratch. I had properties filled with employees and friends, so I ended up having a lot of problems with former employees and former friends. When you think about property management, you're really thinking about efficiency. If your exit strategy is Airbnb rather than a long-term rental and you've got some excess cash to have someone manage this complex property for you, I would highly recommend you do so. I run my local rentals, but I let someone else run my Airbnb business. It's not worth the hassle and the margins work out better when I just step back and let a pro handle it.

Finally, you need to think about strategy overall. I'm long term. I'm not short term. I don't care so much about using cash flow to pay bills. I use cash flow to buy more properties. This helps me avoid having to raise money for every single deal. If you're new, however, short term might be a better strategy to get started. I like cash flow. I like the tax benefits. I like the idea of having 1,000 rentals in order to retire. That's a crazy goal, but I want $500,000-per-month cash flow. That's my North Star. That's why I get up in the morning. But it's attainable, because I have a strategy. When I do short-term deals, it's because they don't work long term, and we can put that short-term money right back into the business to fuel that larger goal. For me, it's about generational wealth. It's the foundation to my legacy, so generations after me will live off the work I do in my thirties, forties, and fifties. Look at your strategy in the same way. Otherwise, what's the point? Why learn all of this if you're not going to use it to change things for your family and better serve your community?

Serve Your Community

"I saw on Instagram you can help with creative finance," a Realtor messaged me on Instagram. Early on, not long after I met Eileen, I started to share my experience on social media. I felt like a caveman who discovered fire, so I needed to spread the message to anyone and everyone who would listen. Ironically, it led to more deals. I started telling people, "If you run into a listing you can't move or a wholesale deal that doesn't work or a house with no equity, let me know." Then I would pay them a finder's fee if I could make the deal work. Now I've done hundreds of deals thanks to my online platform. We've done creative finance, subject-to, seller finance, and everything else you can imagine, because most people don't even know they exist.

This Realtor contacted me with a particularly complex situation. A Realtor has about six months to sell a listed property and one was coming up on that deadline, so the agent reached out to me. The seller had no equity and they had recently done a cash-out refinance. The agent was friends with the seller, so they felt an obligation to help out, even if they lost their cut of the deal. It was five and a half months into the six-month listing agreement and their relationship was getting heated.

Dave, the seller, was building another house, so he had to sell the original house in the next two weeks. He thought he'd lose his deposit on the build. He thought he was in a situation he couldn't get out of, because he thought he couldn't qualify for both mortgages. When the Realtor called me to fix this problem, she told me the house was worth $399,000 but Dave owed $385,000 on the mortgage. Basically, for people in this situation, the traditional method requires them to write a check just to sell the house. Crazy, right? There's not enough cushion for closing costs and Realtor fees and all that other BS that comes with a traditional deal. Most people think he has about $14,000 in equity, but 3 percent is the listing agent's commission, another 3 percent goes to the buyer's agent, and so on. We tell people to assume they're going to pay out about 11 percent for these fees, which in this case is just over $44,000. Steep. Ridiculous. But, ironically, normal.

Someone selling a house for $399,000 using the traditional route is only going to get about $355,000 for it in the end. This means that with a Realtor, he would have had to cut a check just to get out of the deal and qualify for another mortgage. This is why creative finance allows for you to step in like Superman and create a win-win-win scenario. I told the agent I could help and that I'd hook them up with a referral fee if I could make it work. When I finally got to talk to Dave, I explained the situation. Yes, he had no equity, so he'd have to cut a check to work with the Realtor, and that's a bad deal. But I could solve the problem, fix the deal, and even repair this relationship between the Realtor and seller.

"Dave, I can buy your house subject-to, which means I can take over your current Wells Fargo mortgage." Dave said he couldn't do that because he thought he couldn't qualify for two loans at the same time. This is what his lender told him. This is what everybody has told him. "I've been doing this for a while," I told him. "I know how to essentially wipe out your debt-to-income ratio on this house so you can qualify for your new house."

He'd never heard of this before. He repeated what I said in the form of a question. "You can wipe out my debt on this house?"

"Yes, we can wipe out your debt, you keep your name on the house you're trying to sell, and you qualify for the new loan. It's called subject-to."

He didn't believe me, but that's expected.

"Let's get into an agreement," I told him. "We'll open escrow and I will help you get qualified for the other house. Meanwhile, we'll keep your existing mortgage in your name and I'll buy the house." Dave told me that if I could make that work, he would do the deal. "No money out of your pocket," I said, reminding him he didn't really have another option at that point.

I didn't have a contract on me, so I called my wife and she met me at Dave's house to close the deal. We have done this countless times, but I could tell something was different with my wife. She walked into the house and she just looked different. She had this weird face. I had never seen it before. We got into the paperwork and answered all of Dave's follow-up questions, but I was wondering what was going on with Laura. We finished up the paperwork, shook hands with a much-relieved Dave, and exited together

I couldn't stand it anymore. I had to ask her what was up. "What's that expression? What was that face about in there?" I asked her. She looked at me, finally changing her expression, and said, "I want to live in that house."

I can't explain why, but I never thought to personally do a creative finance deal for myself before that moment. It just didn't register for whatever reason. Laura put that idea in my mind, just like she did in the F-150 story. (Like I said before, my wife is a genius.) And that's what we did. We bought our first home subject-to, and it was a game changer for me.

Steve Jobs said, "You can't connect the dots looking forward; you can only connect them looking backwards." When I look back and connect the dots that led me to where I am today, to this book I am writing for you, that led me to help share my epiphanies with you, I realize that I wouldn't change a thing. If I could go back, I would make the same mistakes all over again because I know where those mistakes will lead me. I know that I made huge mistakes. I know that I will continue to make huge mistakes. But that's life. That's business. That's what helped me build everything I have today.

However, the funny thing is that some of the most prolific investors today don't even understand these options. That's why I feel all of this happened for a reason. I'm supposed to be this vessel. That was the $1 million lesson and I have now shared it with you. And now it's your turn to go out there and continue the message. And it all starts with your community.

The Go-Giver Life

The secret to success is service. If you join my mentorship, or even if you just follow me online, I expect you to be a Go-Giver. This comes from the book by the same name from John David Mann and Bob Burg. Being a Go-Giver means going the extra mile. No matter where you are in your business, if you consistently show up and help other people, success is in your future. This is a relationships business, so building those relationships through service is everything. Show up. Ask questions. Answer questions. Help more-experienced people find leads. In exchange, you'll learn everything you need to know about the business and make the connections you need to succeed. You have to want others to win in order to win for yourself (don't worry, we want you to win too—that's how it works).

The idea, of course, comes from the phrase "go-getter," but if you're merely a go-getter, you can be aggressively enterprising in a negative manner. This is why some people hate billionaires. They think of every billionaire as the equivalent of Mr. Burns from *The Simpsons*. They think every billionaire is just out for profit regardless of what problems that might cause. Have there been dozens or hundreds of these people in real life? Of course, but casting down those around you rather than lifting everyone else up is no way to live. If you are equally passionate as the "go-getter" and willing to give more than you get, you can build up everyone around you. This is why we work with group homes. This is why I built an online community. This is why I wrote this book.

The Go-Giver book tells the story of an ambitious young man named Joe. Like many young, smart people, Joe craves success. But, like many new people who are chasing a goal, Joe continues to fall short time and time again. The harder he works, the further his goals appear to be. But, after a particularly bad quarter, Joe is introduced to a consultant who takes him on a journey to meet successful people whom he later describes as Go-Givers. These five people represent the Five Laws of Stratospheric Success. To summarize the Charles Dickens–like story, Joe learns to move his focus from getting to giving, or putting others' interests first and then continuing to add more and more value to their lives.

I met a lot of go-getters early in my career before I started to see the Go-Givers. But the further I got into business, the more Go-Givers I started to meet. Eileen Brown. Jerry Norton. Jamil Damji. Brent Daniels. These people cared about value. These people cared about compensation. These people cared about influence. These people cared about authenticity. These people cared about the law of receptivity. They all had values from this book and they all helped me along the way.

I don't have a direct origin story as to why this message struck me so hard, but it became so clear as I met more and more empathetic business owners who were willing to serve. If you've read this far into this book, I encourage you to become a Go-Giver. It's the only way to build a legacy worth building. It's also the reason why I didn't fold when I faced pitfalls in the beginning. Too many people were counting on me. And now the same type of people are counting on you.

CREATING ACCOUNTABILITY

I want to teach you how to put yourself in a position where you have no choice but to do the right thing. It's time to cut the safety net and get to work. It's time to alter your environment, your way of thinking, and your day-to-day focus. I'm talking about creating accountability that leads to inevitable success. This is how you grow. This is how you serve.

When I was doing construction, businesses like Opendoor found me because I was posting online about our jobs. I was using social media as a tool, and I'm still doing so. One way or another, social media is how you found this book. I had built a reputation around town as the guy who would fund deals and always get the job done. That's who I wanted to be, and it's how I wanted to run my business. But what I didn't expect about this reputation is that suddenly all of these opportunities would turn into obligations. I abandoned any idea of the nine-to-five life and that mythical concept of "work-life balance" and stepped into a 24-7 mindset that embraces "work-life harmony."

In addition to this internal moral compass, I had social pressure. I had built a reputation, and I couldn't suddenly turn around and say, "Sorry, guys, I'm shutting this down. I lost." It wasn't in my nature as an individual, but honestly, I had too many people counting on me in one way or another. To this day, if you come to Arizona, you will not find a single person who said Pace Morby burned them on a deal. I had about 30,000 followers and over 250 employees counting on me to make payroll. I had a family, and we were looking to put down roots. I needed to be a provider.

Here's your challenge. How can you create accountability to take action every single day, even when consistency gets boring and you're in a thirty- or ninety-day plateau? People wish to avoid it, but accountability works. When you publicly commit to something, you have a higher chance of achieving that goal. When someone joins my Facebook community, I encourage them to introduce themselves, talk about their goals, and even share their battle plan. We're not just meeting online to talk and not grow. That's why I created challenges like Zero to Hero and the Get Your First Deal Challenge. When you add accountability to your life, you're increasing your odds of success because you instinctively don't want to be seen as a liar or a failure. Will you make mistakes? Of course. Will you fail? Of course, but not forever. A setback is not the same as a true failure. And if you're worried about whether or not you will have setbacks and make mistakes, don't worry, because you will. You will mess up. It's inevitable. But the more mistakes you overcome, the more likely you are to succeed.

When you create accountability, you also create an unfair advantage. The mere fact that most people avoid accountability is another reason to add it to your life. You need people to hold you accountable. You need to hold others accountable. This is how you serve. I've never been involved in an Alcoholics Anonymous–like program, but I've read that the people who make it to the last step and start to serve others are the ones who make it. They're the least likely to fall off the wagon, because people are counting on them. These people know it takes action one day at a time, and that it's so easy to slip and quit. It's so easy to stop and give up, but when people are counting on you, you can do so much more than you ever thought you were capable of doing.

INVESTOR STORY

Mamadou Diallo—Stop Foreclosure Auction
"Network with a knowledge-based community . . ."

Mamadou Diallo was about to quit real estate before he stumbled across creative finance. He had been doing some wholesale deals but didn't feel like he was serving his communities in the best way with wholesaling alone. When he joined the sub-to community, he knew he could bring more to the table.

Mamadou discovered real estate investing while on a lunch break at his nine-to-five. He had gone through a divorce recently and was about to have his first child. For him, real estate investing was way bigger than real estate. Getting involved with this community and being a problem solver, Mamadou found a new world where he could make a difference. Now several people have gotten their first deal thanks to Mamadou getting involved.

In one of his early deals, he landed a creative finance deal. It was in Texas, and he found it among some other pre-foreclosures. Mamadou likes working with pre-foreclosures because it's possible to help someone's life. In this one, a seller had done a deal with a wholesaler who couldn't perform. The wholesaler left him high and dry one day before his house went up for auction. This sounds insane, but it happens all the time.

Mamadou got a call about this situation. At the time, the seller was mainly confused by what was happening, because the wholesaler had made promises and now it was too late to fix anything or find another cash buyer. This all happened because the wholesaler (who happened to be a licensed agent!) locked in the deal too high and no one wanted to buy, so they wasted thirty days and couldn't find a buyer. The next day, the seller was already planning to move and try to find a temporary living situation.

From Mamadou's perspective, everyone involved up until

this point was only concerned with getting a deal and no one cared what was going to happen to this family that was losing their house. Mamadou jumped in and told them to quit talking about assignment fees and ask the seller what they could do to help out the situation. The bank said there was nothing they could do to hold off the auction.

In the final twenty-four hours before auction, Mamadou found someone in the community to help stop the foreclosure. There are transactional engineers and transactional coordinators who can do this for you in our online community. These professionals can spend three or four hours on the phone to stop a foreclosure auction from taking place.

In this case, since it was early 2022, they first tried a COVID forbearance, but the bank didn't accept it. Then it was auction time in just a few hours. Mamadou and his transaction coordinator were almost out of options. Mamadou considered just wiring over the money, since the seller was only behind $24,000 and Mamadou could make that work. But the wholesaler never opened the title, and since he didn't open escrow (likely because he didn't have the earnest money to deposit!), this option also wouldn't work. Also, since there wasn't a title, there could have been thousands of dollars in liens.

Mamadou told the seller to get in his car and head to the county clerk to file bankruptcy. This was a backup plan to work against the lender and create a case number. The seller is not in bankruptcy, but the application process has begun, and this can pause a foreclosure. The only reason Mamadou knew to do this was because he had joined a network of people to figure out how to handle these types of situations.

About two minutes before the auction, the transaction coordinator got confirmation from the lender that they could push the foreclosure and they would give them thirty more days to figure out how to save the house.

After everything stopped, Mamadou called the seller to learn about his situation. He learned the guy was an ex–car salesman and also a handyman. He also learned that the next day was his twin sons' birthday and he was thrilled that he could get this day and two more weeks in the home (this was part of the new deal they agreed to with Mamadou). Mamadou said he would give the seller $1,400 in cash that day of an eventual $15,000 to walk away. Plus, he helped find a few people to help clean up the property for the seller.

The seller was so grateful to meet Mamadou. The property was worth around $350,000, and the seller just gave him the property. They didn't need to negotiate any further. Mamadou had come in and helped this person when no one else was willing to do so. In a situation like this, it's all about creating some breathing room for the seller, finding out their true situation, and working to create a win-win scenario.

KEY TAKEAWAY | There are always going to be tools that you don't know, but when you show up trying to help and think of the seller first, you will also find yourself in a powerful position.

CHAPTER 16

Next Steps in Your Journey

"I like when money makes a difference but don't make you different."

—DRAKE, "FROM TIME"

If you've read this entire book and not made a single phone call or not gotten in the car to look for deals or not posted something online, then we've both made a mistake. It's time to take action. It's time to toss your hat into the ring. Across my mentorship and social media channels, I've noticed some commonalities among those who make it and those who don't.

First is consistency, but what does that really mean? Essentially, successful investors do repetitive actions, day in and day out, for a long period of time. If you need a number, know that you don't even have any data until you've done something ninety-one days in a row. Consider that a starting point, but you could get your first deal on day 1 or you could get your first deal on day 92 or day 1,002. It all depends on how fast you grow as an individual, implement fundamental steps, and push onward. You want to be a millionaire? Show me. You want to do deals each month? Show me.

Find Your Oasis

Change your environment and leave the naysayers behind. If you're constantly around people who tell you something is impossible, you're eventually going to believe it yourself. But if you're around people who are chasing goals, finding results, and growing as people, you will grow as well. You may have heard the saying "Your network is your net worth." The biggest hurdle for some people may even be a spouse, so the trick to changing this environment is just to simply find your oasis to put in the work. This might be in the garage making phone calls or driving for dollars in your car. You need to find your place of solitude to put in the reps and do the work to get deals. It's here, in this new environment, that you will start to truly believe in yourself, because you'll be able to back it up. Maybe you haven't done a deal yet (results), but you've successfully made calls for twenty-five days in a row (process); you can start to call yourself an investor. If you don't believe in yourself, who will?

What else will help you shift your mindset? Avoid complaints, feeling offended, and victim mentalities. I can't stand complainers. I can't stand people who feel offended all the time and I can't handle victim mentalities. If you think, "Everybody is out to get me," or waste time shouting, "This person took advantage of me," you're not going to make it. It's not about the statement being true or false, it's about the mindset behind the statement. Wealthy, accountable people don't get offended by little things. It goes back to believing in yourself, despite the odds, despite whatever roadblocks appear. Instead of blaming others, think, "How can I fix this problem going forward? Did I set expectations for the deal? Did I fail to communicate? Did I do everything I could to make things work?" Take ownership of your life and everything else will fall into place. As my buddy Jamil said, "You are not entitled to the result. You are entitled to the work."

Expect to lose more than you win. Whether you prefer a batting average metaphor or a Wayne Gretzky quote, you're going to lose more than you win. It's inevitable. This might mean making hundreds of calls to close one deal or having to try out half a dozen assistants before you find the perfect fit. There's always going to be a little struggle when you're chasing something to build a better system. But here's the good news: When you expect to succeed and plan to fail, you're going to find yourself in the right headspace to keep up the process even when times are slow or results nonexistent. This is how you build momentum despite the elements.

Always push the momentum train forward, even if it's just a few minutes a day in the beginning. To expand on this idea a little more, you should be the one who loves to do the hard things. Here's why: No one wants to do the hard things. That's why they're hard. That's also why they're there. The hard things are your ticket to success, because the line to do the hard things is nonexistent. No one is standing on the hard-work stairs because everyone is looking for the shortcut escalator. It's the simplest barrier to entry. Let everyone else complain and work for someone else. You avoid complaints and work for yourself. As the saying goes, "Eat a live frog first thing in the morning and nothing worse will happen to you the rest of the day." The basic idea here is to do the worst part of your day in the beginning to make the rest of the day easy for you. Don't let hard things loom over you all day. Knock them out as early as possible and always be the one to volunteer to do the hard things.

Finally, compete with yourself. If you do a deal with someone and they make $40,000, but you only make $10,000, you need to cheer them on. It's not just about one deal, but the life span of deals, so don't compete with other people on earnings, only compete with yourself. This isn't saying you can't have accountability partners or healthy competitions, because you should have those things, but you do need to be a better version of yourself, year after year.

My friend Brent Daniels invites a handful of people over each year, and we talk about our previous earnings from the year before, our current goals, and where we plan to take these goals. Brent requires everyone to be brutally honest during these conversations. The group setting creates accountability, but the real competition here is between our past selves, our current selves, and our future selves. Brent tells everyone there that we need to earn at minimum

20 percent more per year in order to get invited back. Accountability plus internal competition is the key to true success. Forget FOMO. Forget the fluff. Focus on your journey. Focus on growth.

Faith without Works

There's a folklore creature known as the Mothman, which flies around tormenting the locals in West Virginia. I guess this is scary, but what's scarier is how many "Mothmen" I see floating around from resource to resource never taking action. They're taking notes. Maybe they're asking questions. But they're not getting their hands dirty. They're not taking on any risk or experiencing any bumps and bruises. This is no way to launch a business. This is no way to be a real estate investor.

In order to start a real estate business, you have to be active and consistent. Be part of it. Don't just be a passive person. Don't worry about being embarrassed. Don't worry about making mistakes—you will make them. That's the only way to grow and learn. If I don't have some anxiety about my business, I get anxiety about the lack of anxiety. You should be uncomfortable. You should have activity going on because you're taking action. You should be out there making mistakes. But you can't float from bright light to bright light and expect your business—or your life—to change.

How do you take action? First, you need to be positive. As you start to join online communities or meet active real estate investors, you're also going to meet people who make more deals than you or close deals faster than you. This happens, but everything balances out. Some people will hit lucky streaks before you do, but that's no reason to let others outwork you. If you're putting in the work, doing the right actions, you will have success. Obsessing over your detailed notes and trying to learn every single little thing before you begin is no way to build a business. Be positive, focus on your process, and the results will come.

Next, you need to improve your environment. What do I mean by this? Where you currently are got you to this point, but that doesn't mean it will take you to the next level. In fact, it won't take you to the next level. More than likely, you've got negative influences around you actively holding you back. Certain "friends" hate to see change, so they encourage you to stay just like you have always been, but this will limit your growth. Instead, you need to surround yourself with like-minded individuals who want to see who you will become.

I recently shared the stage with Tim Grover, who is best known for training Michael Jordan and Kobe Bryant. Grover wrote in his book *Winning*, "Friends sometimes feel threatened by your success. Allies understand that your success doesn't distract from theirs." You need to find allies in the industry. When people ask me how to get started in real estate, I tell them to ditch anyone who is currently holding them back (some of them don't even know this is happening, but it is). Anyone who is not helping you grow should not be in your life. More importantly, who can you find that will help hold you accountable? These are your new friends. These are your allies.

Finally, you need to be consistent. This is not news, but how often do you stick with something beyond the results? How long can you learn to love the plateau? Let's compare the business to getting in shape for a moment. Whether you're putting on muscle or losing fat, you will hit a plateau where you stop seeing results, generally around the six-week mark. This is what breaks most people, even when they've been on a positive streak. This goes back to the importance of focusing on the process and not the results, but there's a mental barrier around process. It's less convincing. That's why you have to convince yourself. You have to manifest what you want, know how you're going to get there, and keep your head down until the light at the end of the tunnel burns on the back of your neck. It sounds tough because you've never done anything that required so much consistency, but this process is the fun part. I promise.

Part of this comes from truly knowing your goals. Some people see me talking about manifesting on social media and think I'm talking about summoning magic. It's not magic. It's not luck. It's a clear focus on the path. I literally call my media company ManifestU.

Manifesting, for me, removes the fogginess of the world so you can focus on the individual path to success. There will be plateaus. There will be small roadblocks and there will be massive failures. None of this matters. As the old proverb goes, "Chop wood. Carry water." Continue the journey despite the results. Then the results will arrive on their own. Consistency, in every single facet of life, is the key to success.

When you're being consistent, you will inevitably find solutions to your problems. When you're overthinking, you will merely find problems for solutions. See the difference? From my marketing business and real estate endeavors, I've discovered that people like to solve problems they don't have. I give them a solution to problem X, but then they come up with problem Y. "Here's how you close a deal in two hours," I tell them. They respond, "But what if I get overwhelmed with too many deals at once?" This is ridiculous, but it's how many people are conditioned to think. It's a limiting belief that everyone is out to get you and nothing will work out. It's the opposite mindset you need to be successful and shedding those beliefs is the only way to take your business from zero to one and beyond. Let everyone else get distracted with wants and desires. You focus on the next critical step and an overall commitment to your goal.

Magnify Your Strengths

Finally, let's talk about focusing on what comes to you naturally. The reason I'm not already retired is because I didn't properly magnify my strengths in the early days of my business. I thought I could do everything myself. I thought I could hire my friends. I thought everyone was as motivated as me. I wish someone had told me at an earlier age that there's a role to play, and it's not all about doing everything.

In the book *Rocket Fuel*, the authors Gino Wickman and Mark Winters describe two key leaders in any business: the visionary and the integrator. I'm a visionary, but I wasted a decade trying to be both a visionary and an integrator. This book talks about those roles and encourages you to pursue the category that fits you best. Double down on what you're good at rather than work on things you're not good at.

If you want to be successful in business or in your marriage or in any partnership, you need to understand your strengths and weaknesses. A visionary is an idea person and leader who focuses on the big picture, problem-solving, and ways to advance the business. An integrator tames the chaos by setting priorities, solving conflicts, and removing obstacles. In my business, I'm the visionary and Cody Barton is the integrator. That's what works best for us, because we naturally fit into those two roles. Cody might come in and say we need money for XYZ, then I go out and build relationships so he can put in the work to solve problems. I'm the face, but he's the backbone.

This is how a partnership works, but this is somewhat high-level thinking. You may not be ready to split a business down the middle in this manner, as it's somewhat simplistic and I'm being overly general, but you do need to know your strengths and weaknesses and build on your strengths. If you have no idea where to start and you're new to business, you need to try out every little piece of the process to figure out who you are and where you fit into your big picture.

Then what? When you figure out your strengths, you have to put in the work to learn to delegate, and it's a constant struggle. You have to find your counterparts. I end up saying, "That's not my job," twelve times a day, because you have to be unapologetic about your role. Don't put that burden on yourself.

I don't want to generate leads. I don't want to manage systems. That's not what inspires me to get up in the morning and get going. I don't want to deal with systems. Cody doesn't want to talk to sellers. Together it is a perfect business match. As we started to accelerate, the distinction only got stronger. I've had this personality my entire life, but I struggled for years, because I was missing this counterpart to help me balance the work necessary to bring my vision to life.

Some of the smartest, hardest-working people I know are not successful because they try to do every little thing themselves. You need to separate tasks in order to elevate. You must split up work in order to figure out your own superpowers and put them into practice.

I guarantee that you already know what you're good at and what you're not good at. How many times have you been given a task that just sat on your plate for weeks or months? If tasks are not natural to your capabilities and what you want to do, you're not going to do them. It's a fact. Not everybody is born to be a closer. Not everybody can moderate a successful system. Most people wear too many hats. You have to realize that your partners are your backbone. You need to study who you are and where you fit into your organization. We all have some of the visionary and the integrator, but what is the dominant part of your personality and your world?

As you get older, you realize that you do have something special, whether it's the ability to teach, the ability to articulate, the ability to tell stories, or the ability to resonate with people on a different level. You learn these skills not because they're built inside of you, but because you worked on them and they snowballed over time. I have always known from a young age that one of my personality traits that made me different was my work ethic. You don't have to be that smart. You don't have to be that articulate. You don't have to be the best closer. But you do have to have a strong work ethic and put in the required daily work whether you feel like it or not.

When you figure out who you are and what you want to become, and then add work ethic to your strength, you can truly become unstoppable. That's how you build a business. That's how you build a legacy. You can't leave a legacy behind if you're not putting in the work day after day. But it's not just doing any work; it's about doing the right work. When you go into the fire, you have to do so knowing you're going to make it happen.

My superpowers are telling stories and seeing things ahead of the curve compared to the average investor, like a chess player planning their strategy several moves ahead of their opponent. But this took me years to figure out, years of experience, of failing, and getting back up to do it all over again. It took a million-dollar bankruptcy and a decade of going down the wrong road. Now it's time to start your journey, to discover your superpower, build your legacy, and get out there and serve other people. The best part is that you don't have to wait. You can start right now, right this moment. Once you understand the basics of creative finance, and the idea that you don't need money or credit or connections, the only thing standing in your way is you. The time has come to get out of your own way, follow a proven path, and become the hero of your own story, the way you were always destined to be.

CHAPTER 17

The Morby Method and Beyond

I'm going to keep coming back to the bunny story. Those bunnies changed things for me. It's funny how such a random, unusual situation changed my life—and now, the lives of those I help who are looking to make a real change.

It's not difficult to find someone's reason for wanting a change, but reasons are just surface-level. "I want to move." That's a reason. "I have a job offer." That's also a reason. But that's not the bunnies. That's not the situation that subconsciously guides their decisions. Most people's reason for investing is to make a little extra money, but why? What's the money for? There's always a deeper meaning; that's the point of storytelling.

When you watch a movie, there's a plot and a theme. The plot is what literally happens in the film. But the theme is the underlying message the storytellers want you to understand. *The Shawshank Redemption* is about a prison break, but it's really about hope. *The Godfather* is about the mafia, but it's really about family. If you overlook the theme (or the bunnies) in business, you won't be as successful as you wish to be.

When I moved from construction to investing full time, I brought an employee named Anna Martinez with me. Today, she handles my flips—maybe you've seen her in my YouTube videos—but at the time, I had to figure out how to explain investing to her. It all came back to the bunnies. When I offered Anna this new role, she went from working customer support to calling probate attorneys, following leads, and looking for deals. It took her about six weeks to wrap her head around what we were doing. Finally, I decided I would have to move her because she didn't understand what I was trying to do. Somewhat backed into a corner, she told me, "I don't understand what we're doing here. Why would anyone sell a house to you for fifty cents on the dollar? Why would anyone do this?" I had shifted my mindset, but not her mindset.

I was trying to explain everything to her in a mathematical, logical way. "Buy the deal for this price, flip it for this price or wholesale it for this price, and then make this amount of profit." But I'd forgotten about the bunnies. We looked at our list of deals, and right at the top of the list was Janney. So I told Anna the story of Janney and the bunnies.

A lightbulb went off.

"Why didn't you start by telling me that story? Why didn't you tell me that's what you were doing? It's not about the numbers. It's not about the houses. It's about the people and their situations."

I told her about six more stories, getting across how each house has its own version of bunnies. That's the job. Once you understand the job, you can start to improve your toolkit to find more bunnies. It's just creative problem-solving and relationship-building. It's never about the house; it's always about the person. And that's what led me to the Morby Method.

The Morby Method

We've gone over a lot of creative finance strategies in this book. You will eventually need all of these strategies to close more deals. I say this because you're in the people-helping business, so the more ways you can help people, the more deals you can close. One deal needs seller finance to work. One deal needs subject-to to work. And so on.

But if you do enough deals and look for enough bunnies, and if you continue to think more creatively, you can come up with your own hybrid models to close even more deals.

In a recent Morby Method deal, a Florida seller named Bill wanted a massive down payment—fifty percent of the deal. The Morby Method was my tool to tackle this particular obstacle. The house was a three-bedroom, two-bath property that I knew I could turn into an Airbnb. But in my call with Bill, he told me, "I have to have this money."

I gave him my usual response, knowing there's only three reasons why anyone needs that much money at once.

"There's three reasons why a seller won't agree to seller finance," I said to Bill. "No. 1: They don't understand how it benefits them, because I've done a poor job telling them the story of how it works. No. 2: They really need the money right now, be it for a surgery or their daughter's wedding. No. 3: They aren't motivated to sell the house in the first place." Bill didn't skip a beat when he told me that he actually did need to pay for a wedding. (I've used the wedding example for years, and it's true more often than you would think!)

That was his reason, and there's a vague bunny in there, but I wanted to go a little deeper. Why is this going to be such an expensive wedding? Why does anyone need $200,000 for a wedding? We kept talking, and Bill told me the truth. He had his daughter at a very young age, and he wasn't around for her in her early life. He'd spent the rest of her life trying to get involved and be there as a father. Around the age of 16, the daughter had started to let him in, and Bill was doing everything he could to work things out.

Even as she let him in, Bill's daughter was skeptical of her father. She was afraid of being abandoned again, and I'm sure he had ups and downs throughout her life. He had his own issues. She blamed herself. And now that both of these people were taking a chance on each other, Bill felt this massive wedding would help resolve things—or, at least, be another step in the right direction for this relationship. For him, this wedding was an opportunity for him to step up and make his daughter whole. He could take care of his daughter one last time as he gave her away to this new man, who could hopefully take care of her better than her father ever could.

Already, this was about much more than a wedding. But beyond that, Bill also wanted the money for a down payment on his daughter's first home—a fresh start for everyone. He told me, "I couldn't be her foundation, so I wanted to buy her a house that has a foundation."

Now, a regular investor who hadn't taken the time to get to the bottom of this would have thought that $200,000 for a wedding (reason) was stupid and there was no deal there. But once I heard this story about this man trying to show up for his daughter (situation), I could say, "I completely understand. How can I help you accomplish that?" I showed up with a strategy, not just the hope to make a deal based on a reason.

THE LOGISTICS OF THE DEAL

Now that you get the bunnies, we can get back to the math. I needed to understand both story and logistics to close the deal. The house was $400,000 in value, and Bill needed $200,000 for the down payment. I decided to commit to solving this problem. First, I could get a loan for $200,000 to solve Bill's problem. Then, Bill would seller carry the back end (the additional $200,000) to make the deal work.

Bill was so thrilled to have this work out that he set up the deal so I wouldn't have to make payments on the second half of the house for a decade. Then I could focus on paying back the $200,000 loan or possibly sell the house in ten years. There are lots of options for the second payment, and I could make that decision based on my overall portfolio and the market in ten years.

The other problem in Bill's deal that I needed to solve was that he wouldn't take less than $400,000 total. It all goes back to the same emotional problem. Bill had made some big mistakes in his life, but he was proud of having bought this property. While cashing in for $300,000 to a wholesaler would fix his problem immediately, he saw this $400,000 in equity as the one thing he'd done right. Selling it for less meant, to Bill, that he was discounting the triumphs in life that got him back on the right track. He needed confirmation that he'd made at least one decision in the right direction. I could give him that confirmation.

Acquisition people think these sellers are greedy, but in reality, these sellers are just trying to solve a problem in their life. They've often got some sort of baggage, and the only solution they have is the equity in their house. If you don't know this going in, you don't understand why they won't budge on their tactic. That's why you need to be willing to show up with a solution. If you are negotiating against what someone believes is their single tool to solve an emotional problem, your negotiations will fail. Find the bunnies. Re-home their problem.

Creating Your Own Methods

This book is merely the beginning. I wrote it for you, and I wrote it for the younger version of myself. I wish someone had handed me this book when I was in high school, bagging groceries or delivering pizzas, so I could have changed the trajectory of my life sooner. But that's not what happened. That's not my story, but maybe it can be your story. Maybe, just maybe, you can use this book to change your life and the lives of those around you, so you can build generational wealth for your family and others.

Even though most of these steps are simple, it's not going to be easy. Believe me. I can teach people what to say in a matter of weeks, but it often takes a year or more for people to change their mindset. You must continually reprogram your brain. *Find the bunnies. Find the bunnies. Find the bunnies.* That has to drown out everything else you're thinking in that moment. You must be present and then know what to look for.

When people on my acquisition team understand this, they often leave to go start their own businesses! It's that impactful. And I'm giving you all of that and more in this book. The question is, how long will it take you to understand this fully? How long will you wait to build a better future?

I look for deals on dead lists and in impossible situations. That's the creative part. The opportunities were there, like pieces of treasure lying in a blue ocean only I could see, and no one else was looking for them. The opportunities are always there. You just need to change your mindset first, and then your vision will change too, allowing the opportunities to appear before you. This is true in real estate, and this is true in life.

Over the years, I have learned a wide variety of creative finance strategies—seller finance, novation agreements, subject-to, liens, hybrid models, The Morby Method—and everything else I needed to build out my toolkit of powerful real estate investing strategies. But the real thing I learned was how to solve unsolvable problems. For me, I looked at success as the best form of vengeance. Yes, it took me a decade to figure this out. But I wouldn't change any of my mistakes, because I'm grateful for the lessons I learned.

You don't need money. You don't need cash. You don't need credit. You don't need credentials. You don't need to beg other people to work with you. You just need to show up willing to help people solve problems and do so in a creative way. All the information you need is here.

That's my favorite part about working with thousands of students. They can take methods it took me decades to learn and apply them within seconds. Better still, they come up with their own creative strategies based on my groundwork, and they figure out more and more ways to help others. As you're finishing this book, understand that you have an opportunity and an obligation to go out there and help people, to look for the bunnies, to build generational wealth for your family, and to teach others how to create wealth without cash.

CHAPTER 18

Common Questions About *CREATIVE FINANCE*

"Are you mad 'cause I'm askin' you 21 questions?"

—50 CENT, "21 QUESTIONS"

I want all of you to stop being "ask-holes." If you've never heard this phrase before, it's someone who asks too many questions and doesn't take enough action. I've been an "ask-hole" myself before, but trust me, you can leave that part of you behind. From now on, I want to limit you to two questions per day. Ask two questions, then apply the answers, make some mistakes, and get to work.

To help you follow this question diet, let's get it out of your system. Here are the most common questions I get about creative finance.

I've got some experience, a little extra money, but very little time. Where do I start?

This describes a ton of investors. Basically, I would tell you to build a team of virtual assistants who can do the bulk of the work for you.

Your job is to figure out where you fit in the pipeline, what you like to do, and your goals as an investor. Let your team do the rest.

I've got no experience, a bit of free time, but very little money. Where do I start?

This also describes a lot of investors. Build a list of foreclosures or pre-foreclosures and go knock doors. It's intimidating, but it's also the cheapest, most reliable way to get started in real estate. The only thing in your way is your mindset.

How do I know if a deal is a creative deal or a wholesale deal?

It depends on the deal, but the real question here is about exit strategies and underwriting. Read over Chapter 6 and Chapter 8 in more detail to learn the best exit strategy/method for your deal and your overall portfolio.

Do I need to have access to the MLS to find unlisted deals?

There are a number of programs you can use to find deals. Using the MLS and working with Unicorn Realtors is just one method. But unlisted deals or great deals generally aren't on the MLS. The majority of our deals come from speaking to homeowners after cold-calling or door knocking. This doesn't mean you can't find a great listed deal, but it's the exception, not the rule.

Can I do creative deals in my state?

I've done creative deals all over the country, so I'm confident you can do creative deals in your state. The trickiest part is finding the right paperwork for your deal. You can speak with title companies and lawyers in your individual state to get the right contracts to protect your deals. You also should set up an LLC beforehand.

How do you negotiate sub-to deals or creative deals?

Read over Chapter 9 for my most common responses to seller questions, but this is something you'll get better at over time. It's taken me years to be a confident closer. Learn the basics and make sure to put your own spin on things in order to close more deals. Become a storyteller, and over time, you'll figure out what works best to negotiate deals.

Do you have a recession-proof strategy?

Everyone should make up their own portfolio in a way that works for them; even when you think you have a perfect plan, you may find that your tastes change over the years. I like to look for cash flowing creative deals, but I also do wholesaling and long-term Airbnbs. In terms of being recession-proof, it's all about building a diverse portfolio that fits your basic needs and having the mindset to keep going even when you feel uncomfortable.

How do I deliver an effective offer when an agent is involved?

I've created a handful of YouTube seller calls where I speak with agents about a deal, but this isn't the norm. You have to figure out a way to get your foot in the door and create some leverage. If the deal has been on the market for months, you have some leverage and can use that to your advantage. Otherwise, if you're brand new, there are better ways to do deals without going through agents. With rare exceptions, most Realtors are going to be obstacles in your journey.

If you were brand-new, what markets would you focus on?

In some of our challenges, we've answered this question by building businesses from scratch. Basically, I would pick the hottest local area to you and focus on foreclosure lists. You can pull these from online programs, go knock doors, or ask title companies for free lists. However, while this seems like a simple question, it really depends on your investor avatar, what you hope to do, and which market you're already in. Look for my Get Your First Deal Challenge or my Zero to Hero Challenge for specific, step-by-step details.

How do I explain sub-to or creative finance to a lawyer or someone else?

Read over Chapter 2 and figure out how to make these stories your own. Creative finance is not overly complicated, but most people make it complicated by trying to explain it the wrong way. It took me years to develop these stories, but I use them every single deal to explain creative finance and to close deals.

What if I lock in a deal and my tenants can't pay the rent?

These days, people are worried about recession and high interest rates—as they have been throughout history. But no matter what is going on in the housing market, rent rates have historically gone up. This is more of a question of how you plan to deal with a tenant who can no longer afford the rent. Part of this is about a proper screening process. The other part is whether you even need to be in this position at all as an individual. You can save money by doing your own property management, but if you're not good in these situations, it's worth the money to have someone do it for you.

Realistically, how much money will it take to get started?

Here's the answer: It depends on what you're trying to do. You can have literally no money and get started as a bird dog. Find deals for other people, build up your skill set, and make a few grand a month. If you have money and want to build a team of VAs, it'll take a few thousand dollars per month to buy lists and pay your team—but a good closer can close 1 out of 50 hot leads, so that should more than pay for your business. Anything else fits somewhere along the spectrum, and then it's about scalability.

Why do I need an LLC if I haven't closed a deal yet?

This is a business, not a hobby. Purchasing your LLC is the first step to building a real business. An LLC not only legitimizes what you're doing but it also protects you when that first deal comes. You don't want to close your first deal and then lose the bulk of your profits to Uncle Sam. Protect yourself with an LLC before you get in over your head.

How can I protect myself from the due-on-sale clause?

I go over the due-on-sale clause a bit in Chapter 13 and what to do when it happens. In short, you need to make sure all your paperwork is filled out correctly; you can also buy due-on-sale clause insurance to protect your investment for a small fee.

What is the best way to start networking?

The best way to network is to lead with value. If you're brand-new to an online group or in a local community, show up with something. Bring a deal to the table, bring a list to the table, bring a financier to the table. You don't have to have everything, but you need to have something. If you truly have nothing, offer to work for free to help someone else who has a pipeline. This is the best way to learn the business.

How many connections do I need to make to close deals?

I've seen someone join my online community with essentially no connections and close a deal—but that's rare, to say the least. In this business, stop thinking so much about shortcuts and start thinking about KPIs. My team closes at a high rate, but we're experienced at doing so. You'll need to figure out your own numbers, and obviously, the more connections you have, the better off you'll be. Build an empire; don't try to get rich overnight.

How can I better help Realtors understand creative finance?

Give them a copy of this book. Again, it's all about stories. Find a few unique stories that work for you and use them over and over again. Craft them. Doctor them. Work on them. Make it where you can explain these concepts to a small child. It's not overly complicated, so don't make it complicated.

How can I learn to underwrite a deal?

There's a difference between comping and underwriting. Comping is for cash deals while underwriting is for creative deals. I go into more detail in Chapter 8, but it's going to be different based on your exit strategy and your creative tool kit. Either way, you'll need to start with the ARV, the mortgage, the PITI, the rent rate, cash flow estimates, and the entry fee. Then it's just moving numbers till you find a win-win solution for everyone.

How can I buy a home if I don't have stable work experience?

Creative finance! All of the ideas in this book are meant to help both new people with no credit and veteran investors looking to scale. The beauty of these methods is that you can buy one house this way or thousands of houses this way. It's all about understanding the seller's situation, building an ongoing system of leads, and then problem-solving.

What is the Morby Method?

The Morby Method is one of the greatest hacks I ever created. The basic idea is to solve a problem for you: A seller wants too much money for the down payment. Let's say the seller is open to seller finance but only with a large down payment (sometimes because there's a Realtor involved who wants their percentage on the deal). To solve this problem, you can either negotiate a better deal or you can provide a large down payment from your lender (70–80 percent) and then borrow the other 20–30 percent from the seller after you set up the massive payment. Now, the seller can set up a seller finance deal.

Is there a maximum amount of money I should provide on a deal?

This really depends on you and your preference, but I've been known to pay tens of thousands of dollars over the asking price to close the deal. The trick, of course, is that it all makes sense in the end. Look at your long-term strategy for any individual portfolio purchase and make sure it adds up in the long run. You still want to be conservative, and you don't want to get a hard money loan where you aren't making payments because of high interest. Run your numbers and make it work. The amount is less important than the cash flow and overall payments.

How should someone approach a potential partner to JV on a deal?

Whenever you approach anyone to JV, you need to show up with something valuable. Whether you already have some leads or you have a potential deal (meaning you've talked to the seller, not just found something on Zillow), show up with value and tell them what you have to offer. Then, you can rely on their networking and prior experiences to help you close the deal. There are countless examples in our online communities to show you how to lead with value and close deals with experienced investors.

What is a sub-tail deal?

I coined the term sub-tail to refer to a sub-to deal that you sell for retail. You can own the property temporarily and then flip it on the retail market.

What is a novation agreement?

A novation agreement is when you take the original contract and replace it with a contract from a third party. A novation is not technically subject-to because you don't close escrow. This is particularly useful when a homeowner wants a bigger piece of the pie and they're willing to wait for payment. I generally give them a set amount, then I take whatever extra we can make when we sell the house retail.

How can I negotiate zero percent interest with a seller and no money down?

It's not impossible, but this is going to be a rare situation to close this type of deal. Generally speaking, your total amount is going to be much higher than asking price, so closing this unicorn deal really just comes down to finding a seller open to the idea and explaining it to the seller in such a way that it's a no-brainer for them.

How can I build a real estate empire?

Simple. Follow the steps in this book. Take action before becoming an expert. Make mistakes. Grow your method and systemize your process. If you can get one deal, you can get thousands of deals. Your empire is waiting to be built. The time to start is now.

Acknowledgments

This book—and much of my career—would not have been possible without the help and guidance of so many people I've met along the way. First of all, I want to thank my wife, Laura, and our family, Asher, Corbin, and Monday. I want to acknowledge my parents, my siblings, and everyone who taught me little keystones along the way.

Janney Munson taught me how to find the bunnies. Bethany Willis taught me how to get out of my own way and become an investor. Eileen Brown taught me there was another way to get into investing. Brandon Turner and the BiggerPockets community taught me how to collaborate with other investors. Jamil Damji and Brent Daniels taught me how to work with others to create an unstoppable brand. Cody Barton helps me every single day to grow my business.

I want to acknowledge New Reach, the marketing team behind subto.com, and ManifestU, the team that helps me grow my social channels. And finally, I want to thank my students for putting in the work and helping me grow my community. Thank you for helping other people make deals and take action.

More from
BiggerPockets Publishing

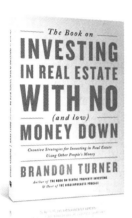

The Book on Investing in Real Estate with No (and Low) Money Down

Is your lack of cash holding you back from your real estate dreams? Discover the creative real estate financing techniques that savvy investors are using to do more deals more often. Longtime cohost of *The BiggerPockets Podcast*, Brandon Turner, dives into multiple financing methods that professional investors use to tap into current real estate markets. Not only will you be able to navigate the world of creative real estate finance, but you'll get more mileage out of any real estate investment strategy!

Real Estate by the Numbers: A Complete Reference Guide to Deal Analysis

Whether you're looking to purchase your first rental property, scale a portfolio, or evaluate massive syndication deals, every great real estate deal comes down to a few key metrics. From cash flow to compound interest, *Real Estate by the Numbers* makes it easy for anyone to master the concepts that form the foundation of real estate investing. J Scott—best-selling author of four business books—and Dave Meyer—VP of Analytics at BiggerPockets—combine their data-driven investing experience to teach you everything you need to analyze deals, track your progress, and think like a professional investor.

If you enjoyed this book, we hope you'll take a moment to check out some of the other great material BiggerPockets offers. Whether you crave freedom or stability, a backup plan, or passive income, BiggerPockets empowers you to live life on your own terms through real estate investing. Find the information, inspiration, and tools you need to dive right into the world of real estate investing with confidence.

Sign up today—it's free! Visit www.BiggerPockets.com
Find our books at www.BiggerPockets.com/store

The Quitter's Manifesto: Quit a Job You Hate for the Work You Love

A life-affirming book for every employee who feels stuck, *The Quitter's Manifesto* is an inspiring guide to leaving a job that doesn't fulfill you in order to find work that does. If you've felt trapped in your job but can't quite seem to take the next step, this book will give you the game plan you need to deal with uncertainty. Written by two successful Quitters and featuring the inspiring stories of many more, this book will help you create a plan that will make leaving a job seem less daunting. The work you love is out there—and your new job is not to give up on yourself.

The Intention Journal

Some people can achieve great wealth, rock-solid relationships, age-defying health, and remarkable happiness—and so many others struggle, fail, and give up on their dreams, goals, and ambitions. Could it simply be that those who find success are more intentional about it? Once you build intentionality into your daily routine, you can achieve the incredible success that sometimes seems out of reach. Backed by the latest research in psychology, this daily planner offers an effective framework to set, review, and accomplish your goals.

HUNGRY FOR MORE
FREE content
ON CREATIVE FINANCE?

Go to
**www.biggerpockets.com
/creativewealth**
for videos, podcast episodes,
blogs, downloadables,
and more.

**Want even more
from BiggerPockets?**

Sign up for a Pro account
and take **20 percent off**
with code **WEALTH20**.

CONNECT WITH BIGGERPOCKETS

Live Life on Your Terms
Through Real Estate Investing!

Facebook
/BiggerPockets

Instagram
@BiggerPockets

Twitter
@BiggerPockets

LinkedIn
/company/Bigger
Pockets

Website
BiggerPockets.com